THE ESSENTIAL

W.S. Merwin

ALSO BY W.S. MERWIN

TRANSLATIONS

Sun at Midnight (poems and letters by Musō Soseki) (with Sōiku Shigematsu)

Collected Haiku of Yosa Buson (with Takako Lento)

Selected Translations 1948–2011

Sir Gawain & the Green Knight

Purgatorio

East Window: The Asian Translations

Pieces of Shadow: Selected Poems of Jaime Sabines

Vertical Poetry (poems by Roberto Juarroz)

From the Spanish Morning

Four French Plays

Selected Translations 1968–1978

Euripedes' Iphigeneia at Aulis (with George E. Dimock Jr.)

Osip Mandelstam: Selected Poems (with Clarence Brown)

Asian Figures

Transparence of the World (poems by Jean Follain)

Voices (poems by Antonio Porchia)

Products of the Perfected Civilization: Selected Writings of Chamfort

Twenty Love Poems and a Song of Despair (poems by Pablo Neruda)

Selected Translations 1948–1968

The Song of Roland

Lazarillo de Tormes

Spanish Ballads

The Satires of Persius

The Poem of the Cid

ANTHOLOGY

Lament for the Makers: A Memorial Anthology

THE ESSENTIAL

W.S. Merwin

EDITED BY MICHAEL WIEGERS

COPPER CANYON PRESS
PORT TOWNSEND, WASHINGTON

Printed in the United States of America

Cover art: Larry C. Cameron, *Merwin Shade House,* copyright 2015

Copper Canyon Press wishes to thank Larry Cameron, Sarah J. Cavanaugh, and Michael Wiegers for their photographs of William and Paula Merwin.

Copper Canyon Press is in residence at Fort Worden State Park in Port Townsend, Washington, under the auspices of Centrum. Centrum is a gathering place for artists and creative thinkers from around the world, students of all ages and backgrounds, and audiences seeking extraordinary cultural enrichment.

LIBRARY OF CONGRESS CATALOGING-IN-PUBLICATION DATA

Names: Merwin, W. S. (William Stanley), 1927– author. | Wiegers, Michael, editor.
Title: The essential W. S. Merwin / W. S. Merwin ; edited by Michael Wiegers.
Description: Port Townsend, Washington : Copper Canyon Press, [2017] | Includes bibliographical references and index.
Identifiers: LCCN 2017004083 | ISBN 9781556595134 (paperback)
Subjects: | BISAC: POETRY / American / General.
Classification: LCC PS3563.E75 A6 2017 | DDC 818/.54—dc23
LC record available at https://lccn.loc.gov/2017004083

987654

Copper Canyon Press
Post Office Box 271
Port Townsend, Washington 98368
www.coppercanyonpress.org

Contents

THE LICE (1967)

Editor's Note

The Essential W.S. Merwin was compiled and edited during particularly urgent times, throughout the world at large as well as in the Merwin household. It is fitting that this be so: through almost seven decades W.S. Merwin's poems have illuminated their tumultuous times, global and domestic, and all the while he has, through his poetry, consistently discovered and created grace.

His output—nearly fifty books of original poems and translations, eight books of prose nonfiction and fiction—is staggering. William Merwin has lived his life singularly, improbably, as a poet. When I first approached the work of distilling his poems to the essential, I had envisioned an impossibly smaller volume. Upon hearing about this project, other poets and readers shared with me their passion for specific poems, and it became clear that hundreds of Merwin's poems have become integral to readers' lives. One thing I have learned through working with William over the past twenty-five years: *listen.* So this book is deeper and more nuanced for that listening.

I also turned, of course, to William and to Paula, his great love and first reader, who was at his side in every endeavor until her death in 2017. I wish she could have seen this book in print; she was critical to its creation and unwavering in her encouragement. Many of the choices within *The Essential* are very much tied to two beloved places that are foundational to Merwin's poetry: their stone cottage and farm buildings in France's Dordogne river valley, and their self-built home in Maui's Pe'ahi watershed near Haiku, Hawaii. I can imagine William walking in his gardens, tools and scraps of writing paper at the ready, looking into the canopy of palms, or across the French river valley, Paula steadily working somewhere nearby.

*

W.S. Merwin has been publishing poems, stories, memoirs, and translations for over sixty-five years—a feat without parallel in American poetry—and what I find remarkable is how the poems are as relevant now as they were at their times of composition. His career spans the globe, and multiple wars—many of which his own country had a hand in, this country that faces repeated periods of civil unrest, denying simultaneously the global environmental devastation that has passed its tipping point. And now, at the later stages of William's life, his poems are shadowed by the returning specter of another authoritarian imperialism. His later poems have embraced courageously his own and Paula's mortality. Looking back at his work over time, one might argue that all of Merwin's writing has been essential.

Starting at home, in each of his gardens, Merwin has been very intentional in how he has planted seedlings, how he then nurtured his plantings. The conditions determined the growth and continuing life he has sought to put back into the world. And yet, he couldn't have completely imagined what those places he tended and stewarded would become. I believe the same holds true for his poetry. Through daily practice and attention, William has created an incredible model for a way of existing on this earth. His poems have defined for future generations what is possible in poetry and in life.

As a reader, I need Merwin's poems. So much so, I've memorized several, including these lines from "Learning a Dead Language":

> What you remember saves you. To remember
> Is not to rehearse, but to hear what never
> Has fallen silent. So your learning is,
> From the dead, order, and what sense of yourself
> Is memorable, what passion may be heard
> When there is nothing for you to say.

MICHAEL WIEGERS
PORT TOWNSEND, WASHINGTON

THE ESSENTIAL

W.S. Merwin

A MASK FOR JANUS

1952

Dictum: For a Masque of Deluge

for Dido

There will be the cough before the silence, then
Expectation; and the hush of portent
Must be welcomed by a diffident music
Lisping and dividing its renewals;
Shadows will lengthen and sway, and, casually
As in a latitude of diversion
Where growth is topiary, and the relaxed horizons
Are accustomed to the trespass of surprise,
One with a mask of Ignorance will appear
Musing on the wind's strange pregnancy.

And to him the one must enter from the south
In a feigned haste, with disaster on his lips,
And tales of distended seas, continents
Submerged, worlds drowned, and of drownings
In mirrors; unto this foreboding
Let them add sidelong but increasing mention,
With darkening syllables, of shadows, as though
They stood and traded restlessness beneath
A gathering dark, until their figures seem
But a flutter of speech down an expense of wind.

So, with talk, like a blather of rain, begun,
Weather will break and the artful world will rush
Incontinent. There must be a vessel.
There must be rummage and shuffling for salvation
Till on that stage and violence, among
Curtains of tempest and shaking sea,
A covered basket, where a child might lie,

Timbered with osiers and floated on a shadow,
Glides adrift, as improbably sailing
As a lotus flower bearing a bull.

Hills are to be forgotten; the patter of speech
Must lilt upon flatness. The beasts will come;
And as they come, let one man, by the ark,
Drunken with desolation, his tongue
Rounding the full statement of the seasons,
Tremble and stare, his eyes seeming to chase
A final clatter of doomed crows, to seek
An affirmation, a mercy, an island,
Or hills crested with towns, and to find only
Cities of cloud already crumbling.

And these the beasts: the bull from the lotus flower
With wings at his shoulders; and a goat, winged;
A serpent undulating in the air;
A lion with wings like falling leaves;
These are to wheel on a winged wheel above
The sullen ark, while hare, swine, crocodile,
Camel, and mouse come; and the sole man, always,
Lurches on childish limbs above the basket—
To his mere humanity seas shall not attain
With tempest, nor the obscure sky with torches.

(Why is it rumored that these beasts come in pairs
When the anatomies of their existence
Are wrought for singularity? They walk
Beside their shadows; their best motions are
Figments on the drapery of the air.
Their propagation is a redoubling
Merely of dark against the wall, a planetary

Leaning in the night unto their shadows
And stiffening to the moment of eclipse;
Shadows will be their lean progeny.)

At last the sigh of recession: the land
Wells from the water; the beasts depart; the man
Whose shocked speech must conjure a landscape
As of some country where the dead years keep
A circle of silence, a drying vista of ruin,
Musters himself, rises, and stumbling after
The dwindling beasts, under the all-colored
Paper rainbow, whose arc he sees as promise,
Moves in an amazement of resurrection,
Solitary, impoverished, renewed.

A falling frond may seem all trees. If so
We know the tone of falling. We shall find
Dictions for rising, words for departure;
And time will be sufficient before that revel
To teach an order and rehearse the days
Till the days are accomplished: so now the dove
Makes assignations with the olive tree,
Slurs with her voice the gestures of the time:
The day foundering, the dropping sun
Heavy, the wind a low portent of rain.

THE DANCING BEARS

1954

On the Subject of Poetry

I do not understand the world, Father.
By the millpond at the end of the garden
There is a man who slouches listening
To the wheel revolving in the stream, only
There is no wheel there to revolve.

He sits in the end of March, but he sits also
In the end of the garden; his hands are in
His pockets. It is not expectation
On which he is intent, nor yesterday
To which he listens. It is a wheel turning.

When I speak, Father, it is the world
That I must mention. He does not move
His feet nor so much as raise his head
For fear he should disturb the sound he hears
Like a pain without a cry, where he listens.

I do not think I am fond, Father,
Of the way in which always before he listens
He prepares himself by listening. It is
Unequal, Father, like the reason
For which the wheel turns, though there is no wheel.

I speak of him, Father, because he is
There with his hands in his pockets, in the end
Of the garden listening to the turning
Wheel that is not there, but it is the world,
Father, that I do not understand.

MISCELLANEOUS TRANSLATIONS

Ja nus hons pris ne dira sa reson

by Richard Coeur de Lion

No prisoner ever said what he was thinking
straight out like someone who suffers nothing
but to ease his mind he can make a song.
My friends are many but are poor at giving.
It is their shame that, with no ransom coming,
these two winters I am held.

They know it well, my barons and my men,
English, Norman, Gascon, and Poitevin:
I never had so poor a companion
that I left him, to save money, in prison.
I say it not to reproach anyone,
but I am still held.

Now I can tell why dead men, as they say,
and prisoners, have no friends or family
since for silver and gold they abandon me.
It hurts me, but hurts my kin still more deeply,
for at my death they will be blamed severely
that I am so long held.

No wonder my heart is sore within me
when my own kin ravages my country.
If he had in mind the promise that we
swore, both of us, to keep mutually
I am certain that I would not long be
here confined and held.

They know full well in Anjou and Touraine,
who at this moment are rich, hale young men,
that I am far, and by strange hands held down.
They love me, but not with one gold grain.
Their splendid arms are missing on the plain
when I have long been held.

Some I have loved and love, comrades of mine,
from Caen some, and some from Percherain,
they tell me, song, cannot be counted on
though my heart toward them never was false or vain.
If they attack me now what a base thing will be done
when I am held.

Countess, sister, may your own sovereign virtue
save you and keep the one this plea is sent to
and by whom I am held.

I say none of this to the heir of Chartrain, who
is Louis's mother.

1948–2008

The Mirabeau Bridge

by Guillaume Apollinaire

Under the Mirabeau Bridge the Seine
Flows and our love
Must I be reminded again
How joy came always after pain

Night comes the hour is rung
The days go I remain

Hands within hands we stand face to face
While underneath
The bridge of our arms passes
The loose wave of our gazing which is endless

Night comes the hour is rung
The days go I remain

Love slips away like this water flowing
Love slips away
How slow life is in its going
And hope is so violent a thing

Night comes the hour is rung
The days go I remain

The days pass the weeks pass and are gone
Neither time that is gone
Nor love ever returns again
Under the Mirabeau Bridge flows the Seine

Night comes the hour is rung
The days go I remain

1956

World's End

by Jean Follain

At the world's end
on worn-out ground
the one talks of the flowers
adorning Argonne china
in their red pigment is mixed
the gold of old Dutch ducats
dissolved in aqua regia.
How soon the night falls
the other answers
time goes so fast
in this empty country.

1967

To a Minor Poet of the Greek Anthology

by Jorge Luis Borges

Where now is the memory
of the days that were yours on earth, and wove
joy with sorrow, and made a universe that was your own?

The river of years has lost them
from its numbered current; you are a word in an index.

To others the gods gave glory that has no end:
inscriptions, names on coins, monuments, conscientious historians;
all that we know of you, eclipsed friend,
is that you heard the nightingale one evening.

Among the asphodels of the Shadow, your shade, in its vanity,
must consider the gods ungenerous.

But the days are a web of small troubles
and is there a greater blessing
than to be the ash of which oblivion is made?

Above other heads the gods kindled
the inexorable light of glory, which peers into the secret parts
        and discovers each separate fault;
glory, that at last shrivels the rose it reveres;
they were more considerate with you, brother.

In the rapt evening that will never be night
you listen without end to Theocritus's nightingale.

1968

The Song of Despair

by Pablo Neruda

The memory of you emerges from the night around me.
The river mingles its stubborn lament with the sea.

Deserted like the wharves at dawn.
It is the hour of departure, oh deserted one!

Cold flower heads are raining over my heart.
Oh pit of debris, fierce cave of the shipwrecked.

In you the wars and the flights accumulated.
From you the wings of the song birds rose.

You swallowed everything, like distance.
Like the sea, like time. In you everything sank!

It was the happy hour of assault and the kiss.
The hour of the spell that blazed like a lighthouse.

Pilot's dread, fury of blind diver,
turbulent drunkenness of love, in you everything sank!

In the childhood of mist my soul, winged and wounded.
Lost discoverer, in you everything sank!

You girdled sorrow, you clung to desire,
sadness stunned you, in you everything sank!

I made the wall of shadow draw back,
beyond desire and act, I walked on.

Oh flesh, my own flesh, woman whom I loved and lost,
I summon you in the moist hour, I raise my song to you.

Like a jar you housed the infinite tenderness,
and the infinite oblivion shattered you like a jar.

There was the black solitude of the islands,
and there, woman of love, your arms took me in.

There were thirst and hunger, and you were the fruit.
There were grief and the ruins, and you were the miracle.

Ah woman, I do not know how you could contain me
in the earth of your soul, in the cross of your arms!

How terrible and brief was my desire of you!
How difficult and drunken, how tensed and avid.

Cemetery of kisses, there is still fire in your tombs,
still the fruited boughs burn, pecked at by birds.

Oh the bitten mouth, oh the kissed limbs,
oh the hungering teeth, oh the entwined bodies.

Oh the mad coupling of hope and force
in which we merged and despaired.

And the tenderness, light as water and as flour.
And the word scarcely begun on the lips.

This was my destiny and in it was the voyage of my longing,
and in it my longing fell, in you everything sank!

Oh pit of debris, everything fell into you,
what sorrow did you not express, in what sorrow are you not drowned!

From billow to billow you still called and sang.
Standing like a sailor in the prow of a vessel.

You still flowered in songs, you still broke in currents.
Oh pit of debris, open and bitter well.

Pale blind diver, luckless slinger,
lost discoverer, in you everything sank!

It is the hour of departure, the hard cold hour
which the night fastens to all the timetables.

The rustling belt of the sea girdles the shore.
Cold stars heave up, black birds migrate.

Deserted like the wharves at dawn.
Only tremulous shadow twists in my hands.

Oh farther than everything. Oh farther than everything.

It is the hour of departure. Oh abandoned one!

1969

Tonight I Can Write

by Pablo Neruda

Tonight I can write the saddest lines.

Write, for example, "The night is starry
and the stars are blue and shiver in the distance."

The night wind revolves in the sky and sings.

Tonight I can write the saddest lines.
I loved her, and sometimes she loved me too.

Through nights like this one I held her in my arms.
I kissed her again and again under the endless sky.

She loved me, sometimes I loved her too.
How could one not have loved her great still eyes.

Tonight I can write the saddest lines.
To think that I do not have her. To feel that I have lost her.

To hear the immense night, still more immense without her.
And the verse falls to the soul like dew to the pasture.

What does it matter that my love could not keep her.
The night is starry and she is not with me.

This is all. In the distance someone is singing. In the distance.
My soul is not satisfied that it has lost her.

My sight tries to find her as though to bring her closer.
My heart looks for her, and she is not with me.

The same night whitening the same trees.
We, of that time, are no longer the same.

I no longer love her, that's certain, but how I loved her.
My voice tried to find the wind to touch her hearing.

Another's. She will be another's. As she was before my kisses.
Her voice, her bright body. Her infinite eyes.

I no longer love her, that's certain, but maybe I love her.
Love is so short, forgetting is so long.

Because through nights like this one I held her in my arms
my soul is not satisfied that it has lost her.

Though this be the last pain that she makes me suffer
and these the last verses that I write for her.

1969

from *Voices*

by Antonio Porchia

Before I travelled my road I was my road.

*

Man goes nowhere. Everything comes to man, like tomorrow.

*

Out of a hundred years a few minutes were made that stayed with me,
     not a hundred years.

*

I have scarcely touched the clay and I am made of it.

*

I know what I have given you. I do not know what you have received.

*

The shadows: some hide, others reveal.

*

My final belief is suffering. And I begin to believe that I do not suffer.

*

When I have nothing left, I will ask for no more.

*

When I throw away what I don't want, it will fall within reach.

1969–88

Asian Figures

Feet of the lantern bearer
move in the dark

(Japanese)

Setting out for the island
forget all your clothes
but not me

(Malay)

Every grave
holds a reason

(Korean)

The hissing starts
in the free seats

(Chinese)

1973

You Have What I Look For

by Jaime Sabines

You have what I look for, what I long for, what I love,
you have it.
The fist of my heart is beating, calling.
I thank the stories for you,
I thank your mother and your father
and death who has not seen you.
I thank the air for you.
You are elegant as wheat,
delicate as the outline of your body.
I have never loved a slender woman
but you have made my hands fall in love,
you moored my desire,
you caught my eyes like two fish.
And for this I am at your door, waiting.

1975

The Lovers

by Jaime Sabines

The lovers say nothing.
Love is the finest of silences,
the one that trembles most and is the hardest to bear.
The lovers are looking for something.
The lovers are the ones who abandon,
the ones who change, who forget.
Their hearts tell them that they will never find.
They don't find, they're looking.

The lovers wander around like crazy people
because they're alone, alone,
surrendering, giving themselves to each moment,
crying because they don't save love.
They worry about love. The lovers
live for the day, it's the best they can do, it's all they know.
They're going away all the time,
all the time, going somewhere else.
They hope,
not for anything in particular, they just hope.
They know that whatever it is, they will not find it.
Love is the perpetual deferment,
always the next step, the other, the other.
The lovers are the insatiable ones,
the ones who must always, fortunately, be alone.

The lovers are the serpents in the story.
They have snakes instead of arms.
The veins in their necks swell
like snakes too, suffocating them.

The lovers can't sleep
because if they do the worms eat them.

They open their eyes in the dark
and terror falls into them.

They find scorpions under the sheet
and their beds float as though on a lake.

The lovers are crazy, only crazy
with no God and no devil.

The lovers come out of their caves
trembling, starving,
chasing phantoms.
They laugh at those who know all about it,
who love forever, truly,
at those who believe in love as an
inexhaustible lamp.

The lovers play at picking up water,
tattooing smoke, at staying where they are.
They play the long sad game of love.
None of them will give up.
The lovers are ashamed to reach any agreement.

Empty, but empty from one rib to another,
death ferments them behind the eyes,
and on they go, they weep toward morning
in the trains, and the roosters wake into sorrow.

Sometimes a scent of newborn earth reaches them,
of women sleeping with a hand on their sex,
contented,
of gentle streams, and kitchens.

The lovers start singing between their lips
a song that is not learned.
And they go on crying, crying
for beautiful life.

1975

Tōki-no Ge (Satori Poem)

by Musō Soseki

Year after year
   I dug in the earth
      looking for the blue of heaven
only to feel
   the pile of dirt
      choking me
until once in the dead of night
   I tripped on a broken brick
      and kicked it into the air
and saw that without a thought
   I had smashed the bones
      of the empty sky

1977–89

"Whenever I sleep"

by Yosa Buson

Whenever I sleep
with my socks on
I have bad dreams

1990–2010
with Takako Lento

Eight Verses on a Humble Life

by Yosa Buson

Stay honest whatever happens
says the bamboo bent under snow
over my window

Wise cuckoo
making no claims
I am a lazy bird in the cold

Here by myself
I put more sticks on the fire
to warm up my soup

The neat folds make
the stuffed paper quilt
look even poorer

A mouse peeps out
its eye on the freezing oil
of my lamp

The charcoal brazier
and the gourd full of charcoal
sit side by side

I can tell my neighbor dislikes me
from the way he clatters his cooking pots
in the cold night

In the night with my few teeth
I try to chew the ice
off the tip of my writing brush

1990–2010

with Takako Lento

"With the sweetness of the new season"

by Guilhem IX, Duke of Aquitane

With the sweetness of the new season
woods fill with leaves and the birds sing
each of them in its own tongue (*en lor lati*)
set to the verse of a new song,
then is the time a man should bring
himself to where his heart has gone.

From my best and fairest to me
no messenger nor seal I see
so my heart neither laughs nor sleeps
nor do I dare take further steps
until I know that we agree
it is as I want it to be.

The way this love of ours goes on
is like the branch of the hawthorn
that keeps trembling upon the tree
in the night in the rain and ice
until the sun comes and the day
spreads through the green leaves and branches.

I can still recall one morning
when we put an end to warring
and how great was the gift she then
gave me: her love and her ring.
God, just let me live to getting
my hand under her cloak again!

What do I care for the strange way
they talk to keep my love away?
I know how words are, how they go
everywhere, one hint is enough.
They talk of love, what do they know?
We have the morsel and the knife.

2001

Quan vei l'alauzeta mover

by Bernart de Ventadorn

When I see how the lark beats
his wings in joy at the sun's ray
when he forgets himself and lets
himself fall with sweetness of heart
oh I feel such envy for
anyone I see in joy
it is a wonder that my heart
does not melt with its desire.

Alas, I knew so much, I thought,
about love, and I knew so little!
For there is no way for me not
to love her who yields none at all.
She took herself and took my heart,
my self and all the world with her,
went and left only desire
and the longing of my heart.

The ladies bring me to despair,
I will not trust them any more.
Long I argued in their favor
but I will not any longer
for none is any use to me
with her who wastes and ruins me.
I have lost faith in all of them
knowing that they are all the same.

Love is lost, that much is certain,
and I never even knew it.

The one in whom it should have been
has none. Where can I look for it?
Oh it looks harsh to those who see her
let this poor creature pine for her
who finds no good except in her,
and die, since no help comes from her.

Since God is no help with my lady
nor mercy, nor what she should give me,
and since it is not her pleasure
to love me, I will never tell her,
and if she rejects and shuns me,
she kills me, and from death I answer.
I will leave, unless she keeps me,
exiled, despairing, who knows where.

I have no will of my own,
nor have been my own since she
let me look into her eyes,
into that mirror that enchants me.
Since in you, mirror, I have seen
myself I perish with deep sighs.
I lost myself there the same way
as fair Narcissus in the fountain.

In this my lady seems like all
the rest, and I blame her for that.
She does not want what she ought to,
and she does what she should not do.
I have crossed the bridge like a fool
and fallen into her ill will.
How it happened I cannot say
unless perhaps I climbed too high.

Tristan, you'll hear no more from me,
I leave and cannot say for where,
sad at heart, and will sing no more
but hide myself from love and joy.

2001

GREEN WITH BEASTS

1956

Leviathan

This is the black sea-brute bulling through wave-wrack,
Ancient as ocean's shifting hills, who in sea-toils
Travelling, who furrowing the salt acres
Heavily, his wake hoary behind him,
Shoulders spouting, the fist of his forehead
Over wastes gray-green crashing, among horses unbroken
From bellowing fields, past bone-wreck of vessels,
Tide-ruin, wash of lost bodies bobbing
No longer sought for, and islands of ice gleaming,
Who ravening the rank flood, wave-marshaling,
Overmastering the dark sea-marches, finds home
And harvest. Frightening to foolhardiest
Mariners, his size were difficult to describe:
The hulk of him is like hills heaving,
Dark, yet as crags of drift-ice, crowns cracking in thunder,
Like land's self by night black-looming, surf churning and trailing
Along his shores' rushing, shoal-water boding
About the dark of his jaws; and who should moor at his edge
And fare on afoot would find gates of no gardens,
But the hill of dark underfoot diving,
Closing overhead, the cold deep, and drowning.
He is called Leviathan, and named for rolling,
First created he was of all creatures,
He has held Jonah three days and nights,
He is that curling serpent that in ocean is,
Sea-fright he is, and the shadow under the earth.
Days there are, nonetheless, when he lies
Like an angel, although a lost angel,
On the waste's unease, no eye of man moving,
Bird hovering, fish flashing, creature whatever
Who after him came to herit earth's emptiness.

Froth at flanks seething soothes to stillness,
Waits; with one eye he watches
Dark of night sinking last, with one eye dayrise
As at first over foaming pastures. He makes no cry
Though that light is a breath. The sea curling,
Star-climbed, wind-combed, cumbered with itself still
As at first it was, is the hand not yet contented
Of the Creator. And he waits for the world to begin.

The Master

Not entirely enviable, however envied;
And early outgrew the enjoyment of their envy,
For other preoccupations, some quite as absurd.
Not always edifying in his action: touchy
And dull by turns, prejudiced, often not strictly
Truthful, with a weakness for petty meddling,
For black sheep, churlish rancors and out-of-hand damning.

The messes he got himself into were of his own devising.
He had all the faults he saw through in the rest of us;
As we have taken pains, and a certain delight, in proving,
Not denying his strength, but still not quite sure where it was;
But luck was with him too, whatever that is,
For his rightful deserts, far from destroying him,
Turned out to be just what he'd needed, and he used them.

Opportunist, shrewd waster, half calculation,
Half difficult child; a phony, it would seem
Even to his despairs, were it not for the work, and that certain
Sporadic but frightening honesty allowed him
By those who loathed him most. Not nice in the home,
But a few loved him. And he loved. Who? What? Some still
Think they know, as some thought they knew then, which is just as well.

In this lifetime what most astonished those
Acquainted with him, was the amount of common
Detail he could muster, and with what intimate ease,
As though he knew it all from inside. For when
Had he seen it? They recalled him as one who most often
Seemed slow, even stupid, not above such things surely,
But absent, with that air maybe part fake, and part shifty.

Yet famously cursed in his disciples:
So many, emulous, but without his unique powers,
Could only ape and exaggerate his foibles.
And he bewildered them as he did no others,
Though they tried to conceal it: for, like mirrors
In a fun-house, they were static, could never keep up with him,
Let alone predict. But stranded on strange shores following him.

So the relief, then the wide despair, when he was gone;
For not only his imitators did he leave feeling
Naked, without voice or manner of their own:
For over a generation his ghost would come bullying
Every hand: all modes seemed exhausted, and he had left nothing
Of any importance for them to do,
While what had escaped him eluded them also.

For only with his eyes could they see, with his ears hear
The world. He had made it. And hard, now, to believe
In the invention: all seems so styleless, as though it had come there
By itself, since the errors and effort are in their grave.
But real: here we are walking in it. Oh, what we can never forgive
Is the way every leaf calls up to our helpless remembrance
Our reality and its insupportable innocence.

Burning the Cat

In the spring, by the big shuck-pile
Between the bramble-choked brook where the copperheads
Curled in the first sun, and the mud road,
All at once it could no longer be ignored.
The season steamed with an odor for which
There has never been a name, but it shouted above all.
When I went near, the wood-lice were in its eyes
And a nest of beetles in the white fur of its armpit.
I built a fire there by the shuck-pile
But it did no more than pop the beetles
And singe the damp fur, raising a stench
Of burning hair that bit through the sweet day-smell.
Then thinking how time leches after indecency,
Since both grief is indecent and the lack of it,
I went away and fetched newspaper,
And wrapped it in dead events, days and days,
Soaked it in kerosene and put it in
With the garbage on a heaped nest of sticks:
It was harder to burn than the peels of oranges,
Bubbling and spitting, and the reek was like
Rank cooking that drifted with the smoke out
Through the budding woods and clouded the shining dogwood.
But I became stubborn: I would consume it
Though the pyre should take me a day to build
And the flames rise over the house. And hours I fed
That burning, till I was black and streaked with sweat;
And poked it out then, with charred meat still clustering
Thick around the bones. And buried it so
As I should have done in the first place, for
The earth is slow, but deep, and good for hiding;
I would have used it if I had understood

How nine lives can vanish in one flash of a dog's jaws,
A car, or a copperhead, and yet how one small
Death, however reckoned, is hard to dispose of.

River Sound Remembered

That day the huge water drowned all voices until
It seemed a kind of silence unbroken
By anything: a time unto itself and still;

So that when I turned away from its roaring, down
The path over the gully, and there were
Dogs barking as always at the edge of town,

Car horns and the cries of children coming
As though for the first time through the fading light
Of the winter dusk, my ears still sang

Like shells with the swingeing current, and
Its flood echoing in me held for long
About me the same silence, by whose sound

I could hear only the quiet under the day
With the land noises floating there far-off and still;
So that even in my mind now turning away

From having listened absently but for so long
It will be the seethe and drag of the river
That I will hear longer than any mortal song.

Learning a Dead Language

There is nothing for you to say. You must
Learn first to listen. Because it is dead
It will not come to you of itself, nor would you
Of yourself master it. You must therefore
Learn to be still when it is imparted,
And, though you may not yet understand, to remember.

What you remember is saved. To understand
The least thing fully you would have to perceive
The whole grammar in all its accidence
And all its system, in the perfect singleness
Of intention it has because it is dead.
You can learn only a part at a time.

What you are given to remember
Has been saved before you from death's dullness by
Remembering. The unique intention
Of a language whose speech has died is order,
Incomplete only where someone has forgotten.
You will find that that order helps you to remember.

What you come to remember becomes yourself.
Learning will be to cultivate the awareness
Of that governing order, now pure of the passions
It composed; till, seeking it in itself,
You may find at last the passion that composed it,
Hear it both in its speech and in yourself.

What you remember saves you. To remember
Is not to rehearse, but to hear what never
Has fallen silent. So your learning is,
From the dead, order, and what sense of yourself

Is memorable, what passion may be heard
When there is nothing for you to say.

Two Paintings by Alfred Wallis

I. *Voyage to Labrador*

Tonight when the sea runs like a sore,
Swollen as hay and with the same sound,
Where under the hat-dark the iron
Ship slides seething, hull crammed
With clamors the fluttering hues of a fever,
Clang-battened in, the stunned bells done
From the rung-down quartans, and only
The dotty lights still trimmed
Abroad like teeth, there dog-hunched will the high
Street of hugging bergs have come
To lean huge and hidden as women,
Untouched as smoke and, at our passing, pleased
Down to the private sinks of their cold.
Then we will be white, all white, as cloths sheening,
Stiff as teeth, white as the sticks
And eyes of the blind. But morning, mindless
And uncaring as Jesus, will find nothing
In that same place but an empty sea
Colorless, see, as a glass of water.

II. *Schooner under the Moon*

Waits where we would almost be. Part
Pink as a tongue; floats high on the olive
Rumpled night-flood, foresails and clouds hiding
Such threat and beauty as we may never see.

The Shipwreck

The tale is different if even a single breath
Escapes to tell it. The return itself
Says survival is possible. And words made to carry
In quiet the burden, the isolation
Of dust, and that fail even so,
Though they shudder still, must shrink the great head
Of elemental violence, the vast eyes
Called blind looking into the ends of darkness,
The mouth deafening understanding with its one
All-wise syllable, into a shriveled
History that the dry-shod may hold
In the palms of their hands. They had her
Under jib and reefed mizzen, and in the dark
Were fairly sure where they were, and with sea-room,
And it seemed to be slacking a little, until
Just before three they struck. Heard
It come home, hollow in the hearts of them,
And only then heard the bell ringing, telling them
It had been ringing there always telling them
That there it would strike home, hollow, in
The hearts of them. Only then heard it
Over the sunlight, the dozing creak
Of the moorings, the bleaching quay, the heat,
The coiled ropes on the quay the day they would sail
And the day before, and across the water blue
As a sky through the heat beyond
The coils, the coils, with their shadows coiled
Inside them. And it sprang upon them dark,
Bitter, and heavy with sound. They began to go
To pieces at once under the waves' hammer.
Sick at heart since that first stroke, they moved

Nevertheless as they had learned always to move
When it should come, not weighing hope against
The weight of the water, yet knowing that no breath
Would escape to betray what they underwent then.
Dazed too, incredulous, that it had come,
That they could recognize it. It was too familiar,
And they in the press of it, therefore, as though
In a drifting dream. But it bore in upon them
Bursting slowly inside them where they had
Coiled it down, coiled it down: this sea, it was
Blind, yes, as they had said, and treacherous—
They had used their own traits to character it—but without
Accident in its wildness, in its rage,
Utterly and from the beginning without
Error. And to some it seemed that the waves
Grew gentle, spared them, while they died of that knowledge.

The Eyes of the Drowned Watch Keels Going Over

Where the light has no horizons we lie.
It dims into depth not distance. It sways
Like hair, then we shift and turn over slightly.
As once on the long swing under the trees
In the drowse of summer we slid to and fro
Slowly in the soft wash of the air, looking
Upward through the leaves that turned over and back
Like hands, through the birds, the fathomless light,
Upward. They go over us swinging
Jaggedly, laboring between our eyes
And the light. Churning their wrought courses
Between the sailing birds and the awed eyes
Of the fish, with the grace of neither, nor with
The stars' serenity that they follow.
Yet the light shakes around them as they go.
Why? And why should we, rocking on shoal-pillow,
With our eyes cling to them, and their wakes follow,
Who follow nothing? If we could remember
The stars in their clarity, we might understand now
Why we pursued stars, to what end our eyes
Fastened upon stars, how it was that we traced
In their remote courses not their own fates but ours.

THE DRUNK IN THE FURNACE

1960

Odysseus

for George Kirstein

Always the setting forth was the same,
Same sea, same dangers waiting for him
As though he had got nowhere but older.
Behind him on the receding shore
The identical reproaches, and somewhere
Out before him, the unravelling patience
He was wedded to. There were the islands
Each with its woman and twining welcome
To be navigated, and one to call "home."
The knowledge of all that he betrayed
Grew till it was the same whether he stayed
Or went. Therefore he went. And what wonder
If sometimes he could not remember
Which was the one who wished on his departure
Perils that he could never sail through,
And which, improbable, remote, and true,
Was the one he kept sailing home to?

Deception Island

for Arthur Mizener

You can go farther. The south itself
Goes much farther, hundreds of miles, first
By sea, then over the white continent,
Mountainous, unmapped, all the way to the pole.

But sometimes imagination
Is content to rest here, at harbor
In the smooth bay in the dead mountain,
Like a vessel at anchor in its own reflection.

The glassy roadstead sleeps in a wide ring
Of ice and igneous shingle, whose gradual
Slopes rise, under streaks of white and black all
The swept shapes of wind, to the volcano's ridges.

It is like being suspended in the open
Vast wreck of a stony skull dead for ages.
You cannot believe the crater was ever
Fiery, before it filled with silence, and sea.

It is not a place you would fancy
You would like to go to. The slopes are barren
Of all the vegetation of desire.
But a place to imagine lying at anchor,

Watching the sea outside the broken
Temple of the cold fire-head, and wondering
Less at the wastes of silence and distance
Than at what all that lonely fire was for.

Fable

However the man had got himself there,
There he clung, kicking in midair,
Hanging from the top branch of a high tree
With his grip weakening gradually.
A passerby who noticed him
Moved a safe distance from under the limb,
And then stood with his arms akimbo, calling,
"Let go, or you'll be killed; the tree is falling."
The man up on the branch, blindly clinging,
With his face toward heaven, and his knees heaving,
Heard this, through his depending to and fro,
And with his last ounce of good faith, let go.
No creature could have survived that fall,
And the stranger was not surprised at all
To find him dead, but told his body, "You
Only let go because you wanted to;
All you lacked was a good reason.
I let you hope you might save your skin
By taking the most comfortable way."
Then added smiling, as he walked away,
"Besides, you'd have fallen anyway."

No One

> Who would it surprise
> If (after the flash, hush, rush,
> Thump, and crumpling) when the wind of prophecy
> Lifts its pitch, and over the drifting ash
> At last the trump splits the sky,
> No One should arise
>
> (No one just as before:
> No limbs, eyes, presence;
> Mindless and incorruptible) to inherit
> Without question the opening heavens,
> To be alone, to be complete,
> And so forever?
>
> Who had kept our secrets,
> Whose wisdom we had heeded,
> Who had stood near us (we proved it) again
> And again in the dark, to whom we had prayed
> Naturally and most often,
> Who had escaped our malice—
>
> No more than equitable
> By No One to be succeeded,
> Who had known our merits, had believed
> Our lies, before ourselves whom we had considered
> And (after ourselves) had loved
> Constantly and well.

Summer

Be of this brightness dyed
Whose unrecking fever
Flings gold before it goes
Into voids finally
That have no measure.

Bird-sleep, moonset,
Island after island,
Be of their hush
On this tide that balance
A time, for a time.

Islands are not forever,
Nor this light again,
Tide-set, brief summer,
Be of their secret
That fears no other.

Plea for a Captive

Woman with the caught fox
By the scruff, you can drop your hopes:
It will not tame though you prove kind,
Though you entice it with fat ducks
Patiently to your fingertips
And in dulcet love enclose it
Do not suppose it will turn friend,
Dog your heels, sleep at your feet,
Be happy in the house,
                              No,

It will only trot to and fro,
To and fro, with vacant eye,
Neither will its pelt improve
Nor its disposition, twisting
The raw song of its debasement
Through the long nights, and in your love,
In your delicate meats tasting
Nothing but its own decay
(As at firsthand I have learned),
                                        Oh,

Kill it at once or let it go.

Pool Room in the Lions Club

I'm sure it must be still the same,
Year after year, the faded room
Upstairs out of the afternoon,
The spidery hands, stalking and cautious
Round and round the airless light,
The few words like the dust settling
Across the quiet, the shadows waiting
Intent and still around the table
For the ivory click, the sleeves stirring,
Swirling the smoke, the hats circling
Remote and hazy above the light,
The board creaking, then hushed again.
Trains from the seaboard rattle past,
And from St. Louis and points west,
But nothing changes their concern,
Hurries or calls them. They must think
The whole world is nothing more
Than their gainless harmless pastime
Of utter patience protectively
Absorbed around one smooth table
Safe in its ring of dusty light
Where the real dark can never come.

Burning Mountain

No blacker than others in winter, but
The hushed snow never arrives on that slope.
An emanation of steam on damp days,
With a faint hiss, if you listen some places,
Yes, and if you pause to notice, an odor,
Even so near the chimneyed city, these
Betray what the mountain has at heart. And all night,
Here and there, popping in and out of their holes
Like groundhogs gone nocturnal, the shy flames.

Unnatural, but no mystery.
Many are still alive to testify
Of the miner who left his lamp hanging
Lit in the shaft and took the lift, and never
Missed a thing till, halfway home to supper
The bells' clangor caught him. He was the last
You'd have expected such a thing from;
The worrying kind, whose old-womanish
Precautions had been a joke for years.

Smothered and silent, for some miles the fire
Still riddles the fissured hill, deviously
Wasting and inextinguishable. They
Have sealed off all the veins they could find,
Thus at least setting limits to it, we trust.
It consumes itself, but so slowly it will outlast
Our time and our grandchildren's, curious
But not unique: there was always one of these
Nearby, wherever we moved, when I was a child.

Under it, not far, the molten core
Of the earth recedes from its thin crust
Which all the fires we light cannot prevent
From cooling. Not a good day's walk above it
The meteors burn out in the air to fall
Harmless in empty fields, if at all.
Before long it practically seemed normal,
With its farms on it, and wells of good water,
Still cold, that should last us, and our grandchildren.

The Drunk in the Furnace

For a good decade
The furnace stood in the naked gully, fireless
And vacant as any hat. Then when it was
No more to them than a hulking black fossil
To erode unnoticed with the rest of the junk-hill
By the poisonous creek, and rapidly to be added
    To their ignorance,

They were afterwards astonished
To confirm, one morning, a twist of smoke like a pale
Resurrection, staggering out of its chewed hole,
And to remark then other tokens that someone,
Cosily bolted behind the eyeholed iron
Door of the drafty burner, had there established
    His bad castle.

Where he gets his spirits
It's a mystery. But the stuff keeps him musical:
Hammer-and-anviling with poker and bottle
To his jugged bellowings, till the last groaning clang
As he collapses onto the rioting
Springs of a litter of car seats ranged on the grates,
    To sleep like an iron pig.

In their tar-paper church
On a text about stoke holes that are sated never
Their Reverend lingers. They nod and hate trespassers.
When the furnace wakes, though, all afternoon
Their witless offspring flock like piped rats to its siren
Crescendo, and agape on the crumbling ridge
    Stand in a row and learn.

THE MOVING TARGET

1963

Home for Thanksgiving

I bring myself back from the streets that open like long
Silent laughs, and the others
Spilled into in the way of rivers breaking up, littered with words,
Crossed by cats and that sort of thing,
From the knowing wires and the aimed windows,
Well this is nice, on the third floor, in back of the billboard
Which says Now Improved and I know what they mean,
I thread my way in and sew myself in like money.

Well this is nice with my shoes moored by the bed
And the lights around the billboard ticking on and off like a beacon,
I have brought myself back like many another crusty
Unbarbered vessel launched with a bottle,
From the bare regions of pure hope where
For a great part of the year it scarcely sets at all,
And from the night skies regularly filled with old movies of my fingers,
Weightless as shadows, groping in the sluices,
And from the visions of veins like arteries, and
From the months of plying
Between can and can, vacant as a pint in the morning,
While my sex grew into the only tree, a joyless evergreen,
And the winds played hell with it at night, coming as they did
Over at least one thousand miles of emptiness,
Thumping as though there were nothing but doors, insisting
"Come out," and of course I would have frozen.

Sunday, a fine day, with my ears wiped and my collar buttoned
I went for a jaunt all the way out and back on
A streetcar and under my hat with the dent settled
In the right place I was thinking maybe—a thought
Which I have noticed many times like a bold rat—
I should have stayed making some of those good women

Happy, for a while at least, Vera with
The eau-de-cologne and the small fat dog named Joy,
Gladys with her earrings, cooking, and watery arms, the one
With the limp and the fancy sheets, some of them
Are still there I suppose, oh no,

I bring myself back avoiding in silence
Like a ship in a bottle.
I bring my bottle.
Or there was thin Pearl with the invisible hair nets, the wind would not
Have been right for them, they would have had
Their times, rugs, troubles,
They would have wanted curtains, cleanings, answers, they would have
Produced families their own and our own, hen friends and
Other considerations, my fingers sifting
The dark would have turned up other
Poverties, I bring myself
Back like a mother cat transferring her only kitten,
Telling myself secrets through my moustache,
They would have wanted to drink ship, sea, and all or
To break the bottle, well this is nice,
Oh misery, misery, misery,
You fit me from head to foot like a good grade suit of longies
Which I have worn for years and never want to take off.
I did the right thing after all.

A Letter from Gussie

If our father were alive
The stains would not be defiling
The walls, nor the splintery porch
Be supported mostly by ants,
The garden, gone to the bad
(Though that was purely Mother's),
Would not have poked through the broken
Window like an arm,
And you would never have dared
Behave toward me in this manner,
Like no gentleman and no brother,
Not even a card at Christmas
Last Christmas, and once again
Where are my dividends?

This is my reward
For remaining with our mother
Who always took your part,
You and your investments
With what she made me give you.
Don't you think I'd have liked
To get away also?
I had the brochures ready
And some nice things that fitted.
After all it isn't as though
You'd ever married. Oh
And the plumbing if I may say so
Would not have just lain down,
And the schoolchildren
Would not keep drilling the teeth
Which I no longer have

With their voices, and each time
I go out with a mouthful of clothespins
The pits of the hoodlums would not be
Dug nearer to the back steps.
Maybe you think my patience
Endures forever, maybe
You think I will die. The goat
If you recall I mentioned
I had for a while, died.
And Mother's canary, I
Won't pretend I was sorry.
Maybe you want me to think
You've died yourself, but I have
My information. I've told
Some people of consequence,
So anything can happen.
Don't say I didn't warn you.
I've looked long enough on the bright side,
And now I'm telling you
I won't stir from Mother's chair
Until I get an answer.
Morning noon and night
Can come and go as they please,
And the man from the funeral parlor
To change the calendars,
But I won't go to bed at all
Unless they come and make me,
And they'll have to bend me flat
Before they can put me away.

Lemuel's Blessing

Let Lemuel bless with the Wolf, which is a
dog without a master, but the Lord hears his
cries and feeds him in the desert.

Christopher Smart: *Jubilate Agno*

You that know the way,
Spirit,
I bless your ears which are like cypresses on a mountain
With their roots in wisdom. Let me approach.
I bless your paws and their twenty nails which tell their own prayer
And are like dice in command of their own combinations.
Let me not be lost.
I bless your eyes for which I know no comparison.
Run with me like the horizon, for without you
I am nothing but a dog lost and hungry,
Ill-natured, untrustworthy, useless.

My bones together bless you like an orchestra of flutes.
Divert the weapons of the settlements and lead their dogs a dance.
Where a dog is shameless and wears servility
In his tail like a banner,
Let me wear the opprobrium of possessed and possessors
As a thick tail properly used
To warm my worst and my best parts. My tail and my laugh bless you.
Lead me past the error at the fork of hesitation.
Deliver me

From the ruth of the lair, which clings to me in the morning,
Painful when I move, like a trap;
Even debris has its favorite positions but they are not yours;
From the ruth of kindness, with its licked hands;

I have sniffed baited fingers and followed
Toward necessities which were not my own: it would make me
A habitué of back steps, faithful custodian of fat sheep;

From the ruth of prepared comforts, with its
Habitual dishes sporting my name and its collars and leashes of vanity;

From the ruth of approval, with its nets, kennels, and taxidermists;
It would use my guts for its own rackets and instruments, to play its own
        games and music;
Teach me to recognize its platforms, which are constructed like scaffolds;

From the ruth of known paths, which would use my feet, tail, and ears
        as curios,
My head as a nest for tame ants,
My fate as a warning.

I have hidden at wrong times for wrong reasons.
I have been brought to bay. More than once.
Another time, if I need it,
Create a little wind like a cold finger between my shoulders, then
Let my nails pour out a torrent of aces like grain from a threshing machine;
Let fatigue, weather, habitation, the old bones, finally,
Be nothing to me,
Let all lights but yours be nothing to me.
Let the memory of tongues not unnerve me so that I stumble or quake.

But lead me at times beside the still waters;
There when I crouch to drink let me catch a glimpse of your image
Before it is obscured with my own.

Preserve my eyes, which are irreplaceable.
Preserve my heart, veins, bones,
Against the slow death building in them like hornets until the place is
      entirely theirs.
Preserve my tongue and I will bless you again and again.

Let my ignorance and my failings
Remain far behind me like tracks made in a wet season,
At the end of which I have vanished,
So that those who track me for their own twisted ends
May be rewarded only with ignorance and failings.
But let me leave my cry stretched out behind me like a road
On which I have followed you.
And sustain me for my time in the desert
On what is essential to me.

Separation

Your absence has gone through me
Like thread through a needle.
Everything I do is stitched with its color.

Noah's Raven

Why should I have returned?
My knowledge would not fit into theirs.
I found untouched the desert of the unknown,
Big enough for my feet. It is my home.
It is always beyond them. The future
Splits the present with the echo of my voice.
Hoarse with fulfillment, I never made promises.

Savonarola

Unable to endure my world and calling the failure God, I will destroy
yours.

Dead Hand

Temptations still nest in it like basilisks.
Hang it up till the rings fall.

Departure's Girl-Friend

Loneliness leapt in the mirrors, but all week
I kept them covered like cages. Then I thought
Of a better thing.

And though it was late night in the city
There I was on my way
To my boat, feeling good to be going, hugging
This big wreath with the words like real
Silver: *Bon Voyage.*

                    The night
Was mine but everyone's, like a birthday.
Its fur touched my face in passing. I was going
Down to my boat, my boat,
To see it off, and glad at the thought.
Some leaves of the wreath were holding my hands
And the rest waved good-bye as I walked, as though
They were still alive.

And all went well till I came to the wharf, and no one.

I say no one, but I mean
There was this young man, maybe
Out of the merchant marine,
In some uniform, and I knew who he was; just the same
When he said to me where do you think you're going,
I was happy to tell him.

But he said to me, it isn't your boat,
You don't have one. I said, it's mine, I can prove it:
Look at this wreath I'm carrying to it,
Bon Voyage. He said, this is the stone wharf, lady,

You don't own anything here.
                              And as I
Was turning away, the injustice of it
Lit up the buildings, and there I was
In the other and hated city
Where I was born, where nothing is moored, where
The lights crawl over the stone like flies, spelling now,
Now, and the same fat chances roll
Their many eyes; and I step once more
Through a hoop of tears and walk on, holding this
Buoy of flowers in front of my beauty,
Wishing myself the good voyage.

Invocation

The day hanging by its feet with a hole
In its voice
And the light running into the sand

Here I am once again with my dry mouth
At the fountain of thistles
Preparing to sing.

The Poem

Coming late, as always,
I try to remember what I almost heard.
The light avoids my eye.

How many times have I heard the locks close
And the lark take the keys
And hang them in heaven.

Vocations

I

Simplicity, if you
Have any time
Where do you spend it?
I tempt you with clear water.
All day I hang out a blue eye. All night
I long for the sound of your small bell
Of an unknown metal.

II

Seeing how it goes
I see how it will be:
The color leaves but the light stays,
The light stays but we cannot grasp it.
We leave the tree rocking its
Head in its hands and we
Go indoors.

III

The locked doors of the night were still sitting in their circle.
I recalled the promises of the bridges.
I got up and made my way
To wash my shadow in the river.
In a direction that was lost
The hands of the water have found tomorrow.

Air

Naturally it is night.
Under the overturned lute with its
One string I am going my way
Which has a strange sound.

This way the dust, that way the dust.
I listen to both sides
But I keep right on.
I remember the leaves sitting in judgment
And then winter.

I remember the rain with its bundle of roads.
The rain taking all its roads.
Nowhere.

Young as I am, old as I am,

I forget tomorrow, the blind man.
I forget the life among the buried windows.
The eyes in the curtains.
The wall
Growing through the immortelles.
I forget silence
The owner of the smile.

This must be what I wanted to be doing,
Walking at night between the two deserts,
Singing.

THE LICE

1967

The Animals

All these years behind windows
With blind crosses sweeping the tables

And myself tracking over empty ground
Animals I never saw

I with no voice

Remembering names to invent for them
Will any come back will one

Saying yes

Saying look carefully yes
We will meet again

The Hydra

No no the dead have no brothers

The Hydra calls me but I am used to it
It calls me Everybody
But I know my name and do not answer

And you the dead
You know your names as I do not
But at moments you have just finished speaking

The snow stirs in its wrappings
Every season comes from a new place

Like your voice with its resemblances

A long time ago the lightning was practicing
Something I thought was easy

I was young and the dead were in other
Ages
As the grass had its own language

Now I forget where the difference falls

One thing about the living sometimes a piece of us
Can stop dying for a moment
But you the dead

Once you go into those names you go on you never
Hesitate
You go on

Some Last Questions

What is the head
          A. Ash
What are the eyes
          A. The wells have fallen in and have
          Inhabitants
What are the feet
          A. Thumbs left after the auction
No what are the feet
          A. Under them the impossible road is moving
          Down which the broken necked mice push
          Balls of blood with their noses
What is the tongue
          A. The black coat that fell off the wall
          With sleeves trying to say something
What are the hands
          A. Paid
No what are the hands
          A. Climbing back down the museum wall
          To their ancestors the extinct shrews that will
          Have left a message
What is the silence
          A. As though it had a right to more
Who are the compatriots
          A. They make the stars of bone

The Last One

Well they made up their minds to be everywhere because why not.
Everywhere was theirs because they thought so.
They with two leaves they whom the birds despise.
In the middle of stones they made up their minds.
They started to cut.

Well they cut everything because why not.
Everything was theirs because they thought so.
It fell into its shadows and they took both away.
Some to have some for burning.

Well cutting everything they came to the water.
They came to the end of the day there was one left standing.
They would cut it tomorrow they went away.
The night gathered in the last branches.
The shadow of the night gathered in the shadow on the water.
The night and the shadow put on the same head.
And it said Now.

Well in the morning they cut the last one.
Like the others the last one fell into its shadow.
It fell into its shadow on the water.
They took it away its shadow stayed on the water.

Well they shrugged they started trying to get the shadow away.
They cut right to the ground the shadow stayed whole.
They laid boards on it the shadow came out on top.
They shone lights on it the shadow got blacker and clearer.
They exploded the water the shadow rocked.
They built a huge fire on the roots.
They sent up black smoke between the shadow and the sun.

The new shadow flowed without changing the old one.
They shrugged they went away to get stones.

They came back the shadow was growing.
They started setting up stones it was growing.
They looked the other way it went on growing.
They decided they would make a stone out of it.
They took stones to the water they poured them into the shadow.
They poured them in they poured them in the stones vanished.
The shadow was not filled it went on growing.
That was one day.

The next day was just the same it went on growing.
They did all the same things it was just the same.
They decided to take its water from under it.
They took away water they took it away the water went down.
The shadow stayed where it was before.
It went on growing it grew onto the land.
They started to scrape the shadow with machines.
When it touched the machines it stayed on them.
They started to beat the shadow with sticks.
Where it touched the sticks it stayed on them.
They started to beat the shadow with hands.
Where it touched the hands it stayed on them.
That was another day.

Well the next day started about the same it went on growing.
They pushed lights into the shadow.
Where the shadow got onto them they went out.
They began to stomp on the edge it got their feet.
And when it got their feet they fell down.
It got into eyes the eyes went blind.

The ones that fell down it grew over and they vanished.
The ones that went blind and walked into it vanished.
The ones that could see and stood still
It swallowed their shadows.
Then it swallowed them too and they vanished.
Well the others ran.

The ones that were left went away to live if it would let them.
They went as far as they could.
The lucky ones with their shadows.

The Gods

If I have complained I hope I have done with it

I take no pride in circumstances but there are
Occupations
My blind neighbor has required of me
A description of darkness
And I begin I begin but

All day I keep hearing the fighting in the valley
The blows falling as rice and
With what cause
After these centuries gone and they had
Each their mourning for each of them grief
In hueless ribbons hung on walls
That fell
Their moment
Here in the future continues to find me
Till night wells up through the earth

I
Am all that became of them
Clearly all is lost

The gods are what has failed to become of us
Now it is over we do not speak

Now the moment has gone it is dark
What is man that he should be infinite
The music of a deaf planet
The one note
Continues clearly this is

The other world
These strewn rocks belong to the wind
If it could use them

The River of Bees

In a dream I returned to the river of bees
Five orange trees by the bridge and
Beside two mills my house
Into whose courtyard a blind man followed
The goats and stood singing
Of what was older

Soon it will be fifteen years

He was old he will have fallen into his eyes

I took my eyes
A long way to the calendars
Room after room asking how shall I live

One of the ends is made of streets
One man processions carry through it
Empty bottles their
Image of hope
It was offered to me by name

Once once and once
In the same city I was born
Asking what shall I say

He will have fallen into his mouth
Men think they are better than grass

I return to his voice rising like a forkful of hay

He was old he is not real nothing is real
Nor the noise of death drawing water

We are the echo of the future

On the door it says what to do to survive
But we were not born to survive
Only to live

The Widow

How easily the ripe grain
Leaves the husk
At the simple turning of the planet

There is no season
That requires us

Masters of forgetting
Threading the eyeless rocks with
A narrow light

In which ciphers wake and evil
Gets itself the face of the norm
And contrives cities

The Widow rises under our fingernails
In this sky we were born we are born

And you weep wishing you were numbers
You multiply you cannot be found
You grieve
Not that heaven does not exist but
That it exists without us

You confide
In images in things that can be
Represented which is their dimension you
Require them you say This
Is real and you do not fall down and moan

Not seeing the irony in the air

Everything that does not need you is real

The Widow does not
Hear you and your cry is numberless

This is the waking landscape
Dream after dream after dream walking away through it
Invisible invisible invisible

December Night

The cold slope is standing in darkness
But the south of the trees is dry to the touch

The heavy limbs climb into the moonlight bearing feathers
I came to watch these
White plants older at night
The oldest
Come first to the ruins

And I hear magpies kept awake by the moon
The water flows through its
Own fingers without end

Tonight once more
I find a single prayer and it is not for men

Glimpse of the Ice

I am sure now
A light under the skin coming nearer
Bringing snow
Then at nightfall a moth has thawed out and is
Dripping against the glass
I wonder if death will be silent after all
Or a cry frozen in another age

Provision

All morning with dry instruments
The field repeats the sound
Of rain
From memory
And in the wall
The dead increase their invisible honey
It is August
The flocks are beginning to form
I will take with me the emptiness of my hands
What you do not have you find everywhere

For the Anniversary of My Death

Every year without knowing it I have passed the day
When the last fires will wave to me
And the silence will set out
Tireless traveller
Like the beam of a lightless star

Then I will no longer
Find myself in life as in a strange garment
Surprised at the earth
And the love of one woman
And the shamelessness of men
As today writing after three days of rain
Hearing the wren sing and the falling cease
And bowing not knowing to what

In the Winter of My Thirty-Eighth Year

It sounds unconvincing to say *When I was young*
Though I have long wondered what it would be like
To be me now
No older at all it seems from here
As far from myself as ever

Waking in fog and rain and seeing nothing
I imagine all the clocks have died in the night
Now no one is looking I could choose my age
It would be younger I suppose so I am older
It is there at hand I could take it
Except for the things I think I would do differently
They keep coming between they are what I am
They have taught me little I did not know when I was young

There is nothing wrong with my age now probably
It is how I have come to it
Like a thing I kept putting off as I did my youth

There is nothing the matter with speech
Just because it lent itself
To my uses

Of course there is nothing the matter with the stars
It is my emptiness among them
While they drift farther away in the invisible morning

When You Go Away

When you go away the wind clicks around to the north
The painters work all day but at sundown the paint falls
Showing the black walls
The clock goes back to striking the same hour
That has no place in the years

And at night wrapped in the bed of ashes
In one breath I wake
It is the time when the beards of the dead get their growth
I remember that I am falling
That I am the reason
And that my words are the garment of what I shall never be
Like the tucked sleeve of a one-armed boy

The Asians Dying

When the forests have been destroyed their darkness remains
The ash the great walker follows the possessors
Forever
Nothing they will come to is real
Nor for long
Over the watercourses
Like ducks in the time of the ducks
The ghosts of the villages trail in the sky
Making a new twilight

Rain falls into the open eyes of the dead
Again again with its pointless sound
When the moon finds them they are the color of everything

The nights disappear like bruises but nothing is healed
The dead go away like bruises
The blood vanishes into the poisoned farmlands
Pain the horizon
Remains
Overhead the seasons rock
They are paper bells
Calling to nothing living

The possessors move everywhere under Death their star
Like columns of smoke they advance into the shadows
Like thin flames with no light
They with no past
And fire their only future

When the War Is Over

When the war is over
We will be proud of course the air will be
Good for breathing at last
The water will have been improved the salmon
And the silence of heaven will migrate more perfectly
The dead will think the living are worth it we will know
Who we are
And we will all enlist again

For a Coming Extinction

Gray whale
Now that we are sending you to The End
That great god
Tell him
That we who follow you invented forgiveness
And forgive nothing

I write as though you could understand
And I could say it
One must always pretend something
Among the dying
When you have left the seas nodding on their stalks
Empty of you
Tell him that we were made
On another day

The bewilderment will diminish like an echo
Winding along your inner mountains
Unheard by us
And find its way out
Leaving behind it the future
Dead
And ours

When you will not see again
The whale calves trying the light
Consider what you will find in the black garden
And its court
The sea cows the Great Auks the gorillas
The irreplaceable hosts ranged countless
And foreordaining as stars
Our sacrifices

Join your word to theirs
Tell him
That it is we who are important

Avoiding News by the River

As the stars hide in the light before daybreak
Reed warblers hunt along the narrow stream
Trout rise to their shadows
Milky light flows through the branches
Fills with blood
Men will be waking

In an hour it will be summer
I dreamed that the heavens were eating the earth
Waking it is not so
Not the heavens
I am not ashamed of the wren's murders
Nor the badger's dinners
On which all worldly good depends
If I were not human I would not be ashamed of anything

Watchers

The mowers begin
And after this morning the fox
Will no longer glide close to the house in full day
When a breath stirs the wheat
Leaving his sounds waiting at a distance
Under a few trees

And lie out
Watching from the nodding light the birds on the roofs
The noon sleep

Perhaps nothing
For some time will cross the new size of the stubble fields
In the light
And watch us
But the day itself coming alone
From the woods with its hunger
Today a tall man saying nothing but taking notes
Tomorrow a colorless woman standing
With her reproach and her bony children
Before rain

Looking for Mushrooms at Sunrise

for Jean and Bill Arrowsmith

When it is not yet day
I am walking on centuries of dead chestnut leaves
In a place without grief
Though the oriole
Out of another life warns me
That I am awake

In the dark while the rain fell
The gold chanterelles pushed through a sleep that was not mine
Waking me
So that I came up the mountain to find them

Where they appear it seems I have been before
I recognize their haunts as though remembering
Another life

Where else am I walking even now
Looking for me

THE CARRIER OF LADDERS

1970

Teachers

Pain is in this dark room like many speakers
of a costly set though mute
as here the needle and the turning

the night lengthens it is winter
a new year

what I live for I can seldom believe in
who I love I cannot go to
what I hope is always divided

but I say to myself you are not a child now
if the night is long remember your unimportance
sleep

then toward morning I dream of the first words
of books of voyages
sure tellings that did not start by justifying

yet at one time it seems
had taught me

Words from a Totem Animal

Distance
is where we were
but empty of us and ahead of
me lying out in the rushes thinking
even the nights cannot come back to their hill
any time

*

I would rather the wind came from outside
from mountains anywhere
from the stars from other
worlds even as
cold as it is this
ghost of mine passing
through me

*

I know your silence
and the repetition
like that of a word in the ear of death
teaching
itself
itself
that is the sound of my running
the plea
plea that it makes
which you will never hear
O god of beginnings
immortal

I might have been right
not who I am
but all right
among the walls among the reasons
not even waiting
not seen
but now I am out in my feet and they on their way
the old trees jump up again and again
strangers
there are no names for the rivers
for the days for the nights
I am who I am
O lord cold as the thoughts of birds
and everyone can see me

*

Caught again and held again
again I am not a blessing
they bring me
names
that would fit anything
they bring them to me
they bring me hopes
all day I turn
making ropes
helping

*

My eyes are waiting for me
in the dusk
they are still closed
they have been waiting a long time
and I am feeling my way toward them

*

I am going up stream
taking to the water from time to time
my marks dry off the stones before morning
the dark surface
strokes the night
above its way
There are no stars
there is no grief
I will never arrive
I stumble when I remember how it was
with one foot
one foot still in a name

*

I can turn myself toward the other joys and their lights
but not find them
I can put my words into the mouths
of spirits
but they will not say them
I can run all night and win
and win

*

Dead leaves crushed grasses fallen limbs
the world is full of prayers
arrived at from
afterwards
a voice full of breaking
heard from afterwards
through all
the length of the night

*

I am never all of me
unto myself
and sometimes I go slowly
knowing that a sound one sound
is following me from world
to world
and that I die each time
before it reaches me

*

When I stop I am alone
at night sometimes it is almost good
as though I were almost there
sometimes then I see there is
in a bush beside me the same question
why are you
on this way
I said I will ask the stars
why are you falling and they answered
which of us

*

I dreamed I had no nails
no hair
I had lost one of the senses
not sure which
the soles peeled from my feet and
drifted away
clouds
It's all one
feet
stay mine
hold the world lightly

*

Stars even you
have been used
but not you
silence
blessing
calling me when I am lost

*

Maybe I will come
to where I am one
and find
I have been waiting there
as a new
year finds the song of the nuthatch

*

Send me out into another life
lord because this one is growing faint
I do not think it goes all the way

The Piper

It is twenty years
since I first looked for words
for me now
whose wisdom or something would stay me
I chose to
trouble myself about the onset
of this
it was remote it was grievous
it is true I was still a child

I was older then
than I hope ever to be again
that summer sweating in the attic
in the foreign country
high above the piper but hearing him
once
and never moving from my book
and the narrow
house full of pregnant women
floor above floor
waiting
in that city
where the sun was the one bell

It has taken me till now
to be able to say
even this
it has taken me this long
to know what I cannot say
where it begins
like the names of the hungry

Beginning
I am here
please
be ready to teach me
I am almost ready to learn

Envoy from d'Aubigné

Go book

go
now I will let you
I open the grave
live
I will die for us both

go but come again if you can
and feed me in prison

if they ask you why
you do not boast of me
tell them as they
have forgotten
truth habitually
gives birth in private

Go without ornament
without showy garment
if there is in you any
joy
may the good find it

for the others be
a glass broken in their mouths

Child
how will you
survive with nothing but your virtue
to draw around you
when they shout Die die

who have been frightened before
the many

I think of all I wrote in my time
dew
and I am standing in dry air

Here are what flowers there are
and what hope
from my years

and the fire I carried with me

Book
burn what will not abide your light

When I consider the old ambitions
to be on many lips
meaning little there
it would be enough for me to know
who is writing this
and sleep knowing it

far from glory and its gibbets

and dream of those who drank at the icy fountain
and told the truth

The Gardens of Zuñi

The one-armed explorer
could touch only half of the country
In the virgin half
the house fires give no more heat
than the stars
it has been so these many years
and there is no bleeding

He is long dead with his five fingers
and the sum of their touching
and the memory
of the other hand
his scout

that sent back no message
from where it had reached
with no lines in its palm
while he balanced
balanced
and groped on
for the virgin land

and found where it had been

Little Horse

You come from some other forest
do you
little horse
think how long I have known these
deep dead leaves
without meeting you

I belong to no one
I would have wished for you if I had known how
what a long time the place was empty
even in my sleep
and loving it as I did
I could not have told what was missing

what can I show you
I will not ask you if you will stay
or if you will come again
I will not try to hold you
I hope you will come with me to where I stand
often sleeping and waking
by the patient water
that has no father nor mother

The Night of the Shirts

O pile of white shirts who is coming
to breathe in your shapes to carry your numbers
to appear
what hearts
are moving toward their garments here
their days
what troubles beating between arms

you look upward through
each other saying nothing has happened
and it has gone away and is sleeping
having told the same story
and we exist from within
eyes of the gods

you lie on your backs
and the wounds are not made
the blood has not heard
the boat has not turned to stone
and the dark wires to the bulb
are full of the voice of the unborn

THE MINER'S PALE CHILDREN

1970

The Dwelling

Once when I looked at myself there was nothing. I could not see any size, any shape, any color. I could tell that I was still there because I was frightened, and I could feel that. When I began to think about myself it kept coming down to that, as though that was the only thing to remember. Yes, that was the only thing I could remember about myself clearly and accurately. I was frightened. That one thing went back until I vanished with it. The point of that disappearance could be considered a kind of beginning. And now to the original dread this new fear was added: that I might forget that I was afraid, and so vanish again, entirely.

The new fear was a revelation. It was, so to speak, an addition to my life and I might well have thought of it as a reason for indulging in a moment of precarious rejoicing. But oblivion never left my side. The more I learned the more terrible the possibilities appeared. When I grew too tired to stand up I leaned against a high smooth cliff that ran along a little valley. That way I had a wall at my back. I could tell that I had come to something that was used to staying.

The cliff faced south, across a small stream. The warmth of the day's sunlight remained in the stone after the sun went down. I went back to that place again and again. Because I was frightened I pressed myself against the stone like a being who wants to hide. Sometimes I really wanted to disappear into the cliff. In that one place I thought I might be able to vanish safely. Night after night I spent pressed against the smooth stone. One morning when I woke I saw my shape on it. It stayed there even when I moved away. It was a shadowy form, like the opening of a narrow mouth. I could see my color there on the wall. A kind of shallow darkness. The discovery came to me like a new fear, but I wanted to keep it. I decided not to leave. I spent all day at the cliff wall, pressed hard against it, deepening my shape on it, in my own mind. I even allowed a little of my fear to play at being hope. I stayed there day and night. The age of my wandering without a shape through the shadowy mountains began to seem very remote. A legend. A legend about myself. One day I could feel my appearance itself stirring on the cliff face, turning as the sun went through its course. I knew that my darkness on the wall had sunk into the stone and acquired a shadow of its own. Inside it.

Oblivion came then in the form of a messenger. Sometimes he called himself time, or water. But as soon as he appeared I set him to work. Whatever he told me I answered by becoming more myself. I pressed myself deep into the cliff, where the day never reached. He followed me in. We conversed in silence. At last there were chambers in me, like a heart. And the dust was marked with prints of presences, in the total dark. Some of them were his.

One day I was sure who I was. I left most of my fear in one dark chamber and began to extend outward from the cliff. A wall was built up to the overhanging stone. Other walls rose on either side, and my darkness moved in there, to stay. That day oblivion told me that he was my heir but I told him that I had made up my mind now, I would appear before I disappeared. Even if it made it worse. And I stood there, dark all the way to the outer wall built of separate stones, and was filled with the thought of what I was, and who.

I came to live more and more in the outer room. The inner chambers were a place apart. It seemed to me that the darkness was becoming solid in there. Some of my dreams went on sleeping in there, but places were found for them in the outer room, and in the end most of them moved out and stayed with me. But my fear still spent a great deal of time in there. And I still kept my back to the cliff.

Then one night I grew my own fourth wall, of separate stones. And a roof. Where the cliff had always been. The new stones were not to protect me. To free me. As the work went on I could feel a terrible tremor under me, a remote heaving such as runs through the earth around the roots of an old tree when the wind blows very hard. All of my fear came out of the cliff and joined me, leaving only a ghost of itself in the old place. When the sun rose I stood in the light with four walls. The mountains were far away and were still receding. The cliff was already out of sight. But I could see what I was. I was alone. I was waiting. I had a shadow outside me.

The days move past me now on every side. The birds fly all around me and plunge into the new distances behind me. I have added to the sky. The fear is the same as ever. It is safe now. Even when the roof falls and the walls collapse and the cliff is not even to be thought of and the daylight floods everything and I am forgotten, the fear will survive. Even if it cannot be seen its features will be known, and its existence will be in no doubt. It will be at home everywhere, like oblivion itself. I will not have lived in vain.

Tergvinder's Stone

One time my friend Tergvinder brought a large round boulder into his living room. He rolled it up the steps with the help of some two-by-fours, and when he got it out into the middle of the room, where some people have coffee tables (though he had never had one there himself), he left it. He said that was where it belonged.

It is really a plain-looking stone. Not as large as Plymouth Rock by a great deal, but then it does not have all the claims of a big shaky promotion campaign to support. That was one of the things Tergvinder said about it. He made no claims at all for it, he said. It was other people who called it Tergvinder's Stone. All he said was that according to him it belonged there.

His dog took to peeing on it, which created a problem (Tergvinder had not moved the carpet before he got the stone to where he said it belonged). Their tomcat took to squirting it, too. His wife fell over it quite often at first and it did not help their already strained marriage. Tergvinder said there was nothing to be done about it. It was in the order of things. That was a phrase he seldom employed, and never when he conceived that there was any room left for doubt.

He confided in me that he often woke in the middle of the night, troubled by the ancient, nameless ills of the planet, and got up quietly not to wake his wife, and walked through the house naked, without turning on any lights. He said that at such times he found himself listening, listening, aware of how some shapes in the darkness emitted low sounds like breathing, as they never did by day. He said he had become aware of a hole in the darkness in the middle of the living room, and out of that hole a breathing, a mournful dissatisfied sound of an absence waiting for what belonged to it, for something it had never seen and could not conceive of, but without which it could not rest. It was a sound, Tergvinder said, that touched him with fellow-feeling, and he had undertaken—oh, without saying anything to anybody—to assuage, if he could, that wordless longing that seemed always on the verge of despair. How to do it was another matter, and for months he had circled the problem, night and day, without apparently coming any closer to a solution. Then one day he had seen the stone. It had been there all the time at the bottom of his drive, he said, and he had never really seen it. Never recognized it for what it was. The nearer to the house he had got it, the more certain he had become. The stone had rolled into its present place like a lost loved one falling into arms that had long ached for it.

Tergvinder says that now on nights when he walks through the dark house he comes and stands in the living room doorway and listens to the peace in the middle of the floor. He knows its size, its weight, the touch of it, something of what is thought of it. He knows that it is peace. As he listens, some hint of that peace touches him too. Often, after a while, he steps down into the living room and goes and kneels beside the stone and they converse for hours in silence—a silence broken only by the sound of his own breathing.

Unchopping a Tree

Start with the leaves, the small twigs, and the nests that have been shaken, ripped, or broken off by the fall; these must be gathered and attached once again to their respective places. It is not arduous work, unless major limbs have been smashed or mutilated. If the fall was carefully and correctly planned, the chances of anything of the kind happening will have been reduced. Again, much depends upon the size, age, shape, and species of the tree. Still, you will be lucky if you can get through this stage without having to use machinery. Even in the best of circumstances it is a labor that will make you wish often that you had won the favor of the universe of ants, the empire of mice, or at least a local tribe of squirrels, and could enlist their labors and their talents. But no, they leave you to it. They have learned, with time. This is men's work. It goes without saying that if the tree was hollow in whole or in part, and contained old nests of bird or mammal or insect, or hoards of nuts or such structures as wasps or bees build for their survival, the contents will have to be repaired where necessary, and reassembled, insofar as possible, in their original order, including the shells of nuts already opened. With spiders' webs you must simply do the best you can. We do not have the spider's weaving equipment, nor any substitute for the leaf's living bond with its point of attachment and nourishment. It is even harder to simulate the latter when the leaves have once become dry—as they are bound to do, for this is not the labor of a moment. Also it hardly needs saying that this is the time for repairing any neighboring trees or bushes or other growth that may have been damaged by the fall. The same rules apply. Where neighboring trees were of the same species it is difficult not to waste time conveying a detached leaf back to the wrong tree. Practice, practice. Put your hope in that.

Now the tackle must be put into place, or the scaffolding, depending on the surroundings and the dimensions of the tree. It is ticklish work. Almost always it involves, in itself, further damage to the area, which will have to be corrected later. But as you've heard, it can't be helped. And care now is likely to save you considerable trouble later. Be careful to grind nothing into the ground.

At last the time comes for the erecting of the trunk. By now it will scarcely be necessary to remind you of the delicacy of this huge skeleton. Every motion of the tackle, every slight upward heave of the trunk, the branches, their elaborately re-assembled panoply of leaves (now dead) will draw from you an involuntary gasp. You will watch for a leaf or a twig to be snapped off yet again. You will listen for the nuts to shift in the hollow limb and you will hear whether they are indeed falling into place or are spilling in disorder—in which case, or in the event of anything else of the kind—operations will have to cease, of course, while you correct the matter. The raising itself is no small enterprise, from the moment when the chains tighten around the old bandages until the bole hangs vertical above the stump, splinter above splinter. Now the final straightening of the splinters themselves can take place (the preliminary work is best done while the wood is still green and soft, but at times when the splinters are not badly twisted most of the straightening is left until now, when the torn ends are face to face with each other). When the splinters are perfectly complementary the appropriate fixative is applied. Again we have no duplicate of the original substance. Ours is extremely strong, but it is rigid. It is limited to surfaces, and there is no play in it. However the core is not the part of the trunk that conducted life from the roots up to the branches and back again. It was relatively inert. The fixative for this part is not the same as the one for the outer layers and the bark, and if either of these is involved in the splintered section they must receive applications of the appropriate adhesives. Apart from being incorrect and probably ineffective, the core fixative would leave a scar on the bark.

When all is ready the splintered trunk is lowered onto the splinters of the stump. This, one might say, is only the skeleton of the resurrection. Now the chips must be gathered, and the sawdust, and returned to their former positions. The fixative for the wood layers will be applied to chips and sawdust consisting only of wood. Chips and sawdust consisting of several substances will receive applications of the correct adhesives. It is as well, where possible, to shelter the materials from the elements while working. Weathering makes it harder to identify the smaller fragments. Bark sawdust in particular the earth lays claim to very quickly. You must find your own ways of coping with this problem. There is a certain beauty, you will notice at moments, in the pattern of the chips as they are fitted back into place. You will wonder to what extent it should be described as natural, to what extent man-made. It will lead you on to speculations about the parentage of beauty itself, to which you will return.

The adhesive for the chips is translucent, and not so rigid as that for the splinters. That for the bark and its subcutaneous layers is transparent and runs into the fibers on either side, partially dissolving them into each other. It does not set the sap flowing again but it does pay a kind of tribute to the preoccupations of the ancient thoroughfares. You could not roll an egg over the joints but some of the mineshafts would still be passable, no doubt. For the first exploring insect who raises its head in the tight echoless passages. The day comes when it is all restored, even to the moss (now dead) over the wound. You will sleep badly, thinking of the removal of the scaffolding that must begin the next morning. How you will hope for sun and a still day!

The removal of the scaffolding or tackle is not so dangerous, perhaps, to the surroundings, as its installation, but it presents problems. It should be taken from the spot piece by piece as it is detached, and stored at a distance. You have come to accept it there, around the tree. The sky begins to look naked as the chains and struts one by one vacate their positions. Finally the moment arrives when the last sustaining piece is removed and the tree stands again on its own. It is as though its weight for a moment stood on your heart. You listen for a thud of settlement, a warning creak deep in the intricate joinery. You cannot believe it will hold. How like something dreamed it is, standing there all by itself. How long will it stand there now? The first breeze that touches its dead leaves all seems to flow into your mouth. You are afraid the motion of the clouds will be enough to push it over. What more can you do? What more can you do?

But there is nothing more you can do.
Others are waiting.
Everything is going to have to be put back.

The Eight Cakes

At a given moment in your life eight cakes are being eaten.

The first is in the very country you are in. It is a blood-colored cupcake. It is being raised from a box, on a train, by someone who is used, at last, to your absence.

The second is in another country. It is stone-colored, but iced with nuts and cherries. It is being eaten in the dining room small as an infant greenhouse, though the meals in that family are taken in the unlit kitchen. Plants are standing everywhere, veiling the huge old radio and the piles of magazines. The cake is the first admission of pleasure in that house after the most recent of many deaths. You too have eaten cake from that table but you will not sit down in that room again.

The third is in a third country. It is pale yellow. It is stale. The mice are eating it, in the light of dawn, far above the wide silent water, while in the next room someone long close to you dreams again and again that you are lost.

The fourth is white. Two pieces of it are sitting on a marble table in a crowded tea-room and have not yet been touched by two greedy old ladies, both of whom you have known, who have not seen each other for years. Neither of them will give you a thought. Why should they?

The fifth is in the same country as the second. It is green. It is being eaten by an official whose face you cannot see. He is wearing a flat tie-clasp and no jacket over his nylon shirt. Beside the plate on his desk are documents relating unfavorably to you. He does not like the cake.

The sixth is chocolate. It is being eaten by a child sitting in a chair in which you learned the meaning of "venereal." But the child and you will never meet, and the chair, like the Bourbons, learned nothing.

The seventh is pink. You are eating it yourself out of politeness and boredom, among people who have provided it themselves and whom you will almost certainly never see again.

The eighth is dark purple. The hand that is cutting it drops the knife, and the hand's owner then thinks of you.

A Garden

You are a garden into which a bomb once fell and did not explode, during a war that happened before you can remember. It came down at night. It screamed, but there were so many screams. It was heard, but it was forgotten. It buried itself. It was searched for but it was given up. So much else had been buried alive.

Other bombs fell near it and exploded. You grew older. It slept among the roots of your trees, which fell around it like nets around a fish that supposedly had long since become extinct. In you the rain fell. In your earth the water found the dark egg with its little wings and inquired, but receiving no answer made camp beside it as beside the lightless stones. The ants came to decorate it with their tunnels. In time the grubs slept, leaning against it, and hatched out, hard and iridescent, and climbed away. You grew older, learning from the days and nights.

The tines of forks struck at it from above, and probed, in ignorance. You suffered. You suffer. You renew yourself. Friends gather and are made to feel at home. Babies are left, in their carriages, in your quiet shade. Children play on your grass and lovers lie there in the summer evenings. You grow older, with your seasons. You have become a haven. And one day when a child has been playing in you all afternoon, the pressure of a root or the nose of a mouse or the sleepless hunger of rust will be enough, suddenly, to obliterate all these years of peace, leaving in your place nothing but a crater rapidly filling with time. Then in vain will they look for your reason.

WRITINGS TO AN UNFINISHED ACCOMPANIMENT

1973

Early One Summer

Years from now
someone will come upon a layer of birds
and not know what he is listening for

these are the days
when the beetles hurry through dry grass
hiding pieces of light they have stolen

Song of Man Chipping an Arrowhead

Little children you will all go
but the one you are hiding
will fly

Something I've Not Done

Something I've not done
is following me
I haven't done it again and again
so it has many footsteps
like a drumstick that's grown old and never been used

In late afternoon I hear it come closer
at times it climbs out of a sea
onto my shoulders
and I shrug it off
losing one more chance

Every morning
it's drunk up part of my breath for the day
and knows which way
I'm going
and already it's not done there

But once more I say I'll lay hands on it
tomorrow
and add its footsteps to my heart
and its story to my regrets
and its silence to my compass

A Door

You walk on

carrying on your shoulders
a glass door
to some house that's not been found

there's no handle

you can't insure it
can't put it down

and you pray please let me not
fall please please let
me not drop
it

because you'd drown like water
in the pieces

so you walk on with your hands frozen
to your glass wings
in the wind
while down the door in time with your feet
skies are marching
like water down the inside of a bell

those skies are looking for you
they've left everything
they want you to remember them

they want to write some last phrase
on you
you

but they keep washing off
they need your ears
you can't hear them

they need your eyes
but you can't look up
now

they need your feet oh
they need your feet
to go on

they send out their dark birds for you
each one the last
like shadows of doors calling calling
sailing
the other way

so it sounds like good-bye

The Unwritten

Inside this pencil
crouch words that have never been written
never been spoken
never been taught

they're hiding

they're awake in there
dark in the dark
hearing us
but they won't come out
not for love not for time not for fire

even when the dark has worn away
they'll still be there
hiding in the air
multitudes in days to come may walk through them
breathe them
be none the wiser

what script can it be
that they won't unroll
in what language
would I recognize it
would I be able to follow it
to make out the real names
of everything

maybe there aren't
many
it could be that there's only one word
and it's all we need
it's here in this pencil

every pencil in the world
is like this

Ash

The church in the forest
was built of wood

the faithful carved their names by the doors
same names as ours

soldiers burned it down

the next church where the first had stood
was built of wood

with charcoal floors
names were written in black by the doors
same names as ours

soldiers burned it down

we have a church where the others stood
it's made of ash
no roof no doors

nothing on earth
says it's ours

Sibyl

Your whole age sits between what you hear
and what you write

when you think you're getting younger
it's the voice coming closer
but only to you

so much of your words
is the words
once they've come out of the ground
and you've written them down
on petals
if it's spring

the same wind that tells you everything at once
unstitches your memory
you try to write faster than the thread is pulled
you write straight onto the air
if it's summer

with your empty needle

straight onto a face if there's light enough
straight onto hands
if it's autumn

Horses

The silence of a place where there were once horses
is a mountain

and I have seen by lightning that every mountain
once fell from the air
ringing
like the chime of an iron shoe

high on the cloudy slope
riders who long ago abandoned sadness
leaving its rotting fences and its grapes to fall
have entered the pass
and are gazing into the next valley

I do not see them cross over

I see that I will be lying
in the lightning on an alp of death
and out of my eyes horsemen will be riding

Exercise

First forget what time it is
for an hour
do it regularly every day

then forget what day of the week it is
do this regularly for a week
then forget what country you are in
and practice doing it in company
for a week
then do them together
for a week
with as few breaks as possible

follow these by forgetting how to add
or to subtract
it makes no difference
you can change them around
after a week
both will help you later
to forget how to count

forget how to count
starting with your own age
starting with how to count backward
starting with even numbers
starting with Roman numerals
starting with fractions of Roman numerals
starting with the old calendar
going on to the old alphabet
going on to the alphabet
until everything is continuous again

go on to forgetting elements
starting with water
proceeding to earth
rising in fire

forget fire

Finding a Teacher

In the woods I came on an old friend fishing
and I asked him a question
and he said Wait

fish were rising in the deep stream
but his line was not stirring
but I waited
it was a question about the sun

about my two eyes
my ears my mouth
my heart the earth with its four seasons
my feet where I was standing
where I was going

it slipped through my hands
as though it were water
into the river
it flowed under the trees
it sank under hulls far away
and was gone without me
then where I stood night fell

I no longer knew what to ask
I could tell that his line had no hook
I understood that I was to stay and eat with him

Gift

I have to trust what was given to me
if I am to trust anything
it led the stars over the shadowless mountain
what does it not remember in its night and silence
what does it not hope knowing itself no child of time

what did it not begin what will it not end
I have to hold it up in my hands as my ribs hold up my heart
I have to let it open its wings and fly among the gifts of the unknown
again in the mountain I have to turn
to the morning

I must be led by what was given to me
as streams are led by it
and braiding flights of birds
the gropings of veins the learning of plants
the thankful days
breath by breath

I call to it Nameless One O Invisible
Untouchable Free
I am nameless I am divided
I am invisible I am untouchable
and empty
nomad live with me
be my eyes
my tongue and my hands
my sleep and my rising
out of chaos
come and be given

THE COMPASS FLOWER

1977

The Heart

In the first chamber of the heart
all the gloves are hanging but two
the hands are bare as they come through the door
the bell rope is moving without them
they move forward cupped as though
holding water
there is a bird bathing in their palms
in this chamber there is no color

In the second chamber of the heart
all the blindfolds are hanging but one
the eyes are open as they come in
they see the bell rope moving
without hands
they see the bathing bird
being carried forward
through the colored chamber

In the third chamber of the heart
all the sounds are hanging but one
the ears hear nothing as they come through the door
the bell rope is moving like a breath
without hands
a bird is being carried forward
bathing
in total silence

In the last chamber of the heart
all the words are hanging
but one
the blood is naked as it steps through the door
with its eyes open

and a bathing bird in its hands
and with its bare feet on the sill
moving as though on water
to the one stroke of the bell
someone is ringing without hands

An Encampment at Morning

A migrant tribe of spiders
spread tents at dusk in the rye stubble
come day I see the color
of the planet under their white-beaded tents
where the spiders are bent
by shade fires in damp September
to their live instruments
and I see the color of the planet
when their tents go from above it
as I come that way in a breath cloud
learning my steps
among the tents rising invisibly like the shapes of snowflakes
we are words on a journey
not the inscriptions of settled people

Migration

Prayers of many summers come
to roost on a moment
until it sinks under them
and they resume their journey
flying by night
with the sound
of blood rushing in an ear

Numbered Apartment

In every room rubber bands turn up loose
on dusty surfaces
witnesses

travellers in stopover countries
not knowing a word of the language
each of them
something in particular to do with me
who say laughing that I
was born here one William
on the last day of one September

to whom now it is again a January a Thursday
of an eleven year and
who has forgotten that
day and to whom that week is inaccessible
and this one is plain this
one

and though I say
here
I know it was not
for even at that time it was
ninety-nine streets to the north by the river
and now it is three wars back
and parents gone as though at once

the edifice in the antique
mode of kings of France
to which they took her to give birth
torn down as I
in my name was turning forty-four

and the building did not from that age go alone
into pieces wheeled away
but all through these years
rubber bands have continued to come to me
sometimes many together
arriving to accompany me although
the whole country has changed
means of travel accelerated
signs almost totally replaced traffic re-routed every
love altered
the stamps re-issued and
smells of streets and apples
moved on

the stone city in
the river has changed and of course
the river
and all words even those unread in
envelopes
all those shining cars vanished
after them entire roads gone like kite strings
incalculable records' print grown finer
just the names at that followed by smoke of numbers
and high buildings turned to glass in
other air oh one clear day

I am a different
foot of a same person in the same river
yet rubber bands lead to me and
from me across great distances
I do not recognize them coming nor remember them going
and still they continue to find me and pass like starlight

The Love for October

A child looking at ruins grows younger
but cold
and wants to wake to a new name
I have been younger in October
than in all the months of spring
walnut and may leaves the color
of shoulders at the end of summer
a month that has been to the mountain
and become light there
the long grass lies pointing uphill
even in death for a reason
that none of us knows
and the wren laughs in the early shade now
come again shining glance in your good time
naked air late morning
my love is for lightness
of touch foot feather
the day is yet one more yellow leaf
and without turning I kiss the light
by an old well on the last of the month
gathering wild rose hips
in the sun

HOUSES AND TRAVELLERS

1977

The Lonely Child

The lonely child arranges all his toys in front of him.

"Come, play with me," he says to everyone who comes near. "Come and see all the toys I have."

But they go away.

So he smashes the first of the toys.

Then other children come to watch and help, and to fight over who can break his toys.

If a lonely child has no toys, he makes them.

OPENING THE HAND

1983

Yesterday

My friend says I was not a good son
you understand
I say yes I understand

he says I did not go
to see my parents very often you know
and I say yes I know

even when I was living in the same city he says
maybe I would go there once
a month or maybe even less
I say oh yes

he says the last time I went to see my father
I say the last time I saw my father

he says the last time I saw my father
he was asking me about my life
how I was making out and he
went into the next room
to get something to give me

oh I say
feeling again the cold
of my father's hand the last time

he says and my father turned
in the doorway and saw me
look at my wristwatch and he
said you know I would like you to stay
and talk with me

oh yes I say

but if you are busy he said
I don't want you to feel that you
have to
just because I'm here

I say nothing

he says my father
said maybe
you have important work you are doing
or maybe you should be seeing
somebody I don't want to keep you

I look out the window
my friend is older than I am
he says and I told my father it was so
and I got up and left him then
you know

though there was nowhere I had to go
and nothing I had to do

Questions to Tourists Stopped by a Pineapple Field

Did you like your piece of pineapple   would you like a napkin
who gave you the pineapple   what do you know about them
do you eat much pineapple   where you come from
how did this piece compare   with pineapple you have eaten before
what do you remember about the last time   you ate a piece of pineapple
did you know where it came from   how much did it cost
do you remember the first time   you tasted pineapple
do you like it better fresh   or from the can
what do you remember   of the picture on the can
what did you feel   as you looked at the picture
which do you like better   the picture or the pineapple field
did you ever imagine   pineapples growing somewhere

how do you like   these pineapple fields
have you ever seen   pineapple fields before
do you know whether pineapple   is native to the islands
do you know whether the natives   ate pineapple
do you know whether the natives   grew pineapple
do you know how the land was acquired   to be turned into pineapple fields
do you know what is done to the land   to turn it into pineapple fields
do you know how many months   and how deeply they plow it
do you know what those machines do   are you impressed
do you know what's in those containers   are you interested

what do you think was here   before the pineapple fields
would you suppose that the fields   represent an improvement
do you think they smell better   than they did before
what is your opinion   of those square miles of black plastic
where do you think the plastic   goes when the crop is over
what do you think becomes of the land   when the crop is over
do you think the growers know best   do you think this is for your own good

what and where was the last   bird you noticed
do you remember   what sort of bird it was
do you know whether   there were birds here before
are there any birds   where you come from
do you think it matters   what do you think matters more
have you seen any   natives since you arrived
what were they doing   what were they wearing
what language were they speaking   were they in nightclubs
are there any natives   where you come from

have you taken pictures   of the pineapple fields
would you like for me   to hold the camera
so that you can all   be in the picture
would you mind   if I took your picture
standing in front   of those pineapple fields
do you expect   to come back

what made you decide   to come here
was this what   you came for
when did you first   hear of the islands
where were you then   how old were you
did you first see the islands   in black and white
what words were used   to describe the islands
what do the words mean   now that you are here
what do you do   for a living
what would you say is   the color of pineapple leaves
when you look at things in rows   how do you feel
would you like to dream   of pineapple fields

is this your first visit   how do you like the islands
what would you say   in your own words
you like best   about the islands
what do you want   when you take a trip
when did you get here   how long will you be staying
did you buy any clothes   especially for the islands
how much did you spend on them   before you came
was it easy to find clothes   for the islands
how much have you spent on clothes   since you got here
did you make your own plans   or are you part of a group
would you rather be on your own   or with a group
how many are in your group   how much was your ticket
are the side-tours part of the ticket   or are they extra
are hotel and meals and car   part of the ticket or extra
have you already paid   or will you pay later
did you pay by check   or by credit card
is this car rented   by the day or week
how does it compare   with the one you drive at home
how many miles   does it do to a gallon
how far do you   want to go on this island

where have you been   in the last three hours
what have you seen   in the last three miles
do you feel hurried   on your vacation
are you getting   your money's worth
how old are you   are you homesick are you well
what do you eat here   is it what you want
what gifts are you planning   to take back
how much do you expect   to spend on them
what have you bought   to take home with you
have you decided   where to put each thing
what will you say   about where they came from
what will you say   about the pineapple fields

do you like dancing here   what do you do when it rains
was this trip   purely for pleasure
do you drink more   or less than at home
how do you like   the place where you live now
were you born there   how long have you lived there
what does the name mean   is it a growth community
why are you living there   how long do you expect to stay
how old is your house   would you like to sell it

in your opinion ˌ coming from your background
what do the islands offer   someone of your age
are there any changes   you would like to promote
would you like to invest here   would you like to live here
if so would it be year round   or just for part of the year
do you think there is a future   in pineapple

James

News comes that a friend far away
is dying now

I look up and see small flowers appearing
in spring grass outside the window
and can't remember their name

Berryman

I will tell you what he told me
in the years just after the war
as we then called
the second world war

don't lose your arrogance yet he said
you can do that when you're older
lose it too soon and you may
merely replace it with vanity

just one time he suggested
changing the usual order
of the same words in a line of verse
why point out a thing twice

he suggested I pray to the Muse
get down on my knees and pray
right there in the corner and he
said he meant it literally

it was in the days before the beard
and the drink but he was deep
in tides of his own through which he sailed
chin sideways and head tilted like a tacking sloop

he was far older than the dates allowed for
much older than I was he was in his thirties
he snapped down his nose with an accent
I think he had affected in England

as for publishing he advised me
to paper my wall with rejection slips
his lips and the bones of his long fingers trembled
with the vehemence of his views about poetry

he said the great presence
that permitted everything and transmuted it
in poetry was passion
passion was genius and he praised movement and invention

I had hardly begun to read
I asked how can you ever be sure
that what you write is really
any good at all and he said you can't

you can't you can never be sure
you die without knowing
whether anything you wrote was any good
if you have to be sure don't write

What Is Modern

Are you modern

is the first
tree that comes
to mind modern
does it have modern leaves

who is modern after hours
at the glass door
of the drugstore
or
within sound of the airport

or passing the
animal pound
where once a week I
gas the animals
who is modern in bed

when
was modern born
who first was pleased
to feel modern
who first claimed the word
as a possession
saying I'm
modern

as someone might say
I'm a champion
or I'm
famous or even
as some would say I'm
rich

or I love the sound
of the clarinet
yes so do I
do you like classical
or modern

did modern
begin to be modern
was there a morning
when it was there for the first time
completely modern

is today modern
the modern sun rising
over the modern roof
of the modern hospital
revealing the modern water tanks and aerials
of the modern horizon

and modern humans
one after the other
solitary and without speaking
buying the morning paper
on the way to work

The Black Jewel

In the dark
there is only the sound of the cricket

south wind in the leaves
is the cricket
so is the surf on the shore
and the barking across the valley

the cricket never sleeps
the whole cricket is the pupil of one eye
it can run it can leap it can fly
in its back the moon
crosses the night

there is only one cricket
when I listen

the cricket lives in the unlit ground
in the roots
out of the wind
it has only the one sound

before I could talk
I heard the cricket
under the house
then I remembered summer

mice too and the blind lightning
are born hearing the cricket
dying they hear it
bodies of light turn listening to the cricket
the cricket is neither alive nor dead

the death of the cricket
is still the cricket
in the bare room the luck of the cricket
echoes

THE RAIN IN THE TREES

1988

Late Spring

Coming into the high room again after years
after oceans and shadows of hills and the sounds of lies
after losses and feet on stairs

after looking and mistakes and forgetting
turning there thinking to find
no one except those I knew
finally I saw you
sitting in white
already waiting

you of whom I had heard
with my own ears since the beginning
for whom more than once
I had opened the door
believing you were not far

West Wall

In the unmade light I can see the world
as the leaves brighten I see the air
the shadows melt and the apricots appear
now that the branches vanish I see the apricots
from a thousand trees ripening in the air
they are ripening in the sun along the west wall
apricots beyond number are ripening in the daylight

Whatever was there
I never saw those apricots swaying in the light
I might have stood in orchards forever
without beholding the day in the apricots
or knowing the ripeness of the lucid air
or touching the apricots in your skin
or tasting in your mouth the sun in the apricots

History

Only I never came back

the gates stand open
where I left the barnyard in the evening
as the owl was bringing the mouse home
in the gold sky
at the milking hour
and I turned to the amber hill and followed
along the gray fallen wall
by the small mossed oaks and the bushes of rusting
arches bearing the ripe
blackberries into the long shadow
and climbed the ancient road
through the last songs of the blackbirds

passing the last live farms
their stones running with dark liquid
and the ruined farms their windows without frames
facing away
looking out across the pastures of dead shepherds
whom nobody ever knew
grown high with the dry flowers of late summer
their empty doorways gazing
toward the arms of the last oaks
and at night their broken chimneys watching
the cold of the meteors

the beams had fallen together
to rest in brown herds around the fireplaces
and in the shade of black trees the houses were full
of their own fragrance at last

mushrooms and owls
and the song of the cicadas

there was a note on a page
made at the time
and the book was closed
and taken on a journey
into a country where no one
knew the language

no one could read
even the address
inside the cover
and there the book was
of course lost

it was a book full of words to remember
this is how we manage without them
this is how they manage
without us

I was not going to be long

After School

For a long time I wanted
to get out of that school
where I had been sent
for the best

I thought of climbing
down the vine
outside the window
at night

after the watchman
had turned the corner
to the boiler room
in the sweet autumn dark

I wanted to slip
through the still dining hall
and down the cellar stairs
in the girls' wing

where I had set the waltzing
in the first book
of *War and Peace*
I would pass unseen in that crowd

into the cellar
and the secret door to the steam pipes
and under the street
to the swimming pool

I would have persuaded
a girl I liked

to meet me there
and we would swim whispering

because of the echoes
while the light from the street
shone through the frosted windows
like the light of the moon

all down the hot room
where the sound of the water
made the heart beat loud
to think of it

but I never
got away then
and when I think now
of following that tunnel

there is a black wolf
tied there waiting
a thin bitch
who snaps at my right hand

but I untie her
and we find our way
out of there as one
and down the street

hungry
nobody in sight at that hour
everything closed
behind us

Rain at Night

This is what I have heard

at last the wind in December
lashing the old trees with rain
unseen rain racing along the tiles
under the moon
wind rising and falling
wind with many clouds
trees in the night wind

after an age of leaves and feathers
someone dead
thought of this mountain as money
and cut the trees
that were here in the wind
in the rain at night
it is hard to say it
but they cut the sacred 'ohias then
the sacred koas then
the sandalwood and the halas
holding aloft their green fires
and somebody dead turned cattle loose
among the stumps until killing time

but the trees have risen one more time
and the night wind makes them sound
like the sea that is yet unknown
the black clouds race over the moon
the rain is falling on the last place

The Sound of the Light

I hear sheep running on the path of broken limestone
through brown curled leaves fallen early from walnut limbs
at the end of a summer how light the bony
flutter of their passage I can
hear their coughing their calling and wheezing even the warm
greased wool rubbing on the worn walls I hear them
passing passing in the hollow lane and there is still time

the shuffle of black shoes of women climbing
stone ledges to church keeps flowing up the dazzling hill
around the grassy rustle of voices
on the far side of a slatted shutter
and the small waves go on whispering on the shingle
in the heat of an hour without wind it is Sunday
none of the sentences begins or ends there is time

again the unbroken rumble of trucks and the hiss
of brakes roll upward out of the avenue
I forget what season they are exploding through
what year the drill on the sidewalk is smashing
it is the year in which you are sitting there as you are
in the morning speaking to me and I hear
you through the burning day and I touch you
to be sure and there is time there is still time

Thanks

Listen
with the night falling we are saying thank you
we are stopping on the bridges to bow from the railings
we are running out of the glass rooms
with our mouths full of food to look at the sky
and say thank you
we are standing by the water thanking it
standing by the windows looking out
in our directions

back from a series of hospitals back from a mugging
after funerals we are saying thank you
after the news of the dead
whether or not we knew them we are saying thank you

over telephones we are saying thank you
in doorways and in the backs of cars and in elevators
remembering wars and the police at the door
and the beatings on stairs we are saying thank you
in the banks we are saying thank you
in the faces of the officials and the rich
and of all who will never change
we go on saying thank you thank you

with the animals dying around us
taking our feelings we are saying thank you
with the forests falling faster than the minutes
of our lives we are saying thank you
with the words going out like cells of a brain
with the cities growing over us
we are saying thank you faster and faster
with nobody listening we are saying thank you

thank you we are saying and waving
dark though it is

Place

On the last day of the world
I would want to plant a tree

what for
not for the fruit

the tree that bears the fruit
is not the one that was planted

I want the tree that stands
in the earth for the first time

with the sun already
going down

and the water
touching its roots

in the earth full of the dead
and the clouds passing

one by one
over its leaves

Witness

I want to tell what the forests
were like

I will have to speak
in a forgotten language

Chord

While Keats wrote they were cutting down the sandalwood forests
while he listened to the nightingale they heard their own axes echoing
    through the forests
while he sat in the walled garden on the hill outside the city they thought
    of their gardens dying far away on the mountain
while the sound of the words clawed at him they thought of their wives
while the tip of his pen travelled the iron they had coveted was hateful
    to them
while he thought of the Grecian woods they bled under red flowers
while he dreamed of wine the trees were falling from the trees
while he felt his heart they were hungry and their faith was sick
while the song broke over him they were in a secret place and they were
    cutting it forever
while he coughed they carried the trunks to the hole in the forest the size
    of a foreign ship
while he groaned on the voyage to Italy they fell on the trails and were
    broken
when he lay with the odes behind him the wood was sold for cannons
when he lay watching the window they came home and lay down
and an age arrived when everything was explained in another language

Losing a Language

A breath leaves the sentences and does not come back
yet the old still remember something that they could say

but they know now that such things are no longer believed
and the young have fewer words

many of the things the words were about
no longer exist

the noun for standing in mist by a haunted tree
the verb for I

the children will not repeat
the phrases their parents speak

somebody has persuaded them
that it is better to say everything differently

so that they can be admired somewhere
farther and farther away

where nothing that is here is known
we have little to say to each other

we are wrong and dark
in the eyes of the new owners

the radio is incomprehensible
the day is glass

when there is a voice at the door it is foreign
everywhere instead of a name there is a lie

nobody has seen it happening
nobody remembers

this is what the words were made
to prophesy

here are the extinct feathers
here is the rain we saw

TRAVELS

1993

The Blind Seer of Ambon

I always knew that I came from
another language

and now even when I can no longer see
I continue to arrive at words

but the leaves
and the shells were already here
and my fingers finding them echo
the untold light and depth

I was betrayed into my true calling
and denied in my advancement
I may have seemed somewhat strange
caring in my own time for living things
with no value that we know
languages wash over them one wave at a time

when the houses fell
in the earthquake
I lost my wife
and my daughter
it all roared and stood still
falling
where they were in the daylight

I named for my wife a flower
as though I could name a flower
my wife dark and luminous
and not there

I lost the drawings of the flowers
in fire

I lost the studies
of the flowers
my first six books in the sea

then I saw that the flowers themselves
were gone
they were indeed gone
I saw
that my wife was gone
then I saw that my daughter was gone
afterward my eyes themselves were gone

one day I was looking
at infinite small creatures
on the bright sand
and the next day is this
hearing after music
so this is the way I see now

I take a shell in my hand
new to itself and to me
I feel the thinness the warmth and the cold
I listen to the water
which is the story welling up
I remember the colors and their lives
everything takes me by surprise
it is all awake in the darkness

Rimbaud's Piano

Suddenly at twenty-one
with his poems already behind him
his manuscripts fed to the flames two years
since and his final hope
in the alchemy of the word buried
deep under the dust that chased his blown

soles through Europe and the fine
snows that spun into his slurring footsteps
in the passes southward to Italy
his shoes even then no
longer laced with lyre strings and his fingers
penniless once more then Italy

and its kind widow fading
backward into the darkness and hungers
of London Verlaine's retching and sobbing
the days of the Commune
his Paris dawns bursting for the first time
like poison promising through his blood

there he was back again at
Mother's after all at Mother's and not
even the farm at Roche with its crippled
barn where at least he could
have Hell to himself but the dank little
house on the crabbed street in Charleville

tight curtained like a series
of sickrooms the dimness reeking of walls
and waiting of camphor and vinegar
old bedding and the black

boards of Mother from which he kept turning
to the other door though outside it

there was nothing but Charleville
which he had left he thought and kept leaving
his pockets full of nothing but pages
now from dictionaries
Arabic Hindustani Greek Russian
he was learning them all and teaching

German to the landlord's son
with winter coming on trying to turn
some words into money into numbers
where the future lay but
there must be something to which the numbers
were still witness the harmony

that Pythagoras had called
music in whose continuo the light
burst into bodies knowing everywhere
the notes that were their way
those numbers that were their belonging and
Mother he told her I must have a

piano a piano
he said to her with her blue regard whose
husband had left her and the four children
both daughters sickly one
dying one son from the beginning good
for nothing and this other in whom

she had scrubbed brushed and buttoned
the last of her hopes for this world this one
who had been so good marching before her
to Mass and had won all

the prizes at school this one with the eyes
of ice who could have been anything

and instead had found nothing
better to do than run away like his
brother leaving her and the girls beside
the river telling them
that he was going for a book indeed
and taking the train for Paris with

no ticket letting her guess
what had happened to him with the Germans
advancing on Charleville and her breathless
from door to door searching
in cafés asking for him and all night
rummaging the street looking for him

not for the last time and he
already in the hands of the police
and bad company no wonder after
those books he had brought home
all his studies for nothing wandering
like a tramp with that other and now

a piano and Verlaine
to whom he wrote answered with that vomit
of piety perfected in prison
making it clear that this
long pretext for a loan was merely one
more trick to obtain money whereas

etcetera so he carved
a keyboard on the dining room table
for practicing scales on while he listened
to his pupil's untuned

German and hearkened beyond them both
to the true sound until his mother

out of concern for the
furniture hired a piano which came
on a cart like part of a funeral
to be cursed through the door
as a camel and into its corner
thence to awaken the echoes of

Pythagoras as written
by Mademoiselle Charpentier in her
exercises for the pianoforte
borrowed from the Charleville
choirmaster her notations of those same
intervals that told the distances

among the stars wherefore
they sang stumbling over and over bruised
and shaky all that winter through the sour
rooms while his sister lay
dying while the doors were draped with mourning
before Christmas while the snow fell black

out of the death of the year
into the new the splintered ivory
far from its own vast sufferings sinking
into him daily its
claims so that by spring when he had acquired
a certain noisy proficiency

and the roads melted again
before him into visions of Russia
arches of Vienna faces of thieves
the waiting hands once more

of the police with somewhere beyond them
all a south and its peacock islands

its deserts and the battered
instrument was given up to become
a camel again patient on its own
pilgrimage to the end
of the elephants and its separate
molecules orbiting through unseen

stellar harmonies the drummed
notes of that winter continued to ring
in the heads that heard them they rose through
the oilcloth and the fringed
embroidery that hid the carved keyboard
they echoed the closing of the door

they spiralled after his steps
on the slave routes and slipped out of the first
words of letters from Africa useless
unwelcomed and unloved
without beginning like the trailing knock
of the artificial legs made for

his lost one but never used
heard by no others like the choir of eight
with five principal singers and twenty
orphans who bore candles
at his funeral and meaning nothing
else like the lives through which they sounded

Search Party

By now I know most of the faces
that will appear beside me as
long as there are still images
I know at last what I would choose
the next time if there ever was
a time again I know the days
that open in the dark like this
I do not know where Maoli is

I know the summer surfaces
of bodies and the tips of voices
like stars out of their distances
and where the music turns to noise
I know the bargains in the news
rules whole languages formulas
wisdom that I will never use
I do not know where Maoli is

I know whatever one may lose
somebody will be there who says
what it will be all right to miss
and what is verging on excess
I know the shadows of the house
routes that lead out to no traces
many of his empty places
I do not know where Maoli is

You that see now with your own eyes
all that there is as you suppose
though I could stare through broken glass
and show you where the morning goes
though I could follow to their close

the sparks of an exploding species
and see where the world ends in ice
I would not know where Maoli is

One Story

Always somewhere in the story
which up until now we thought
was ours whoever it was
that we were being then
had to wander out into
the green towering forest
reaching to the end of
the world and beyond older
than anything whoever
we were being could remember
and find there that it was
no different from the story

anywhere in the forest
and never be able to tell
as long as the story was there
whether the fiery voices
now far ahead now under
foot the eyes staring from
their instant that held the story
as one breath the shadows
offering their spread flowers
and the chill that leapt from its own
turn through the hair of the nape
like a light through a forest

knew the untold story
all along and were waiting
at the right place as the moment
arrived for whoever it was
to be led at last by the wiles
of ignorance through the forest

and come before them face
to face for the first time
recognizing them with
no names and again surviving
seizing something alive
to take home out of the story

but what came out of the forest
was all part of the story
whatever died on the way
or was named but no longer
recognizable even
what vanished out of the story
finally day after day
was becoming the story
so that when there is no more
story that will be our
story when there is no
forest that will be our forest

Rain Travel

I wake in the dark and remember
it is the morning when I must start
by myself on the journey
I lie listening to the black hour
before dawn and you are
still asleep beside me while
around us the trees full of night lean
hushed in their dream that bears
us up asleep and awake then I hear
drops falling one by one into
the sightless leaves and I
do not know when they began but
all at once there is no sound but rain
and the stream below us roaring
away into the rushing darkness

Turning

This is the light that I would see again
on the bare stones the puckered fields the roof
this is the light I would long remember
hazed still an afternoon in September
the known voices would be low and feathered
as though crossing water or in the presence
of moment the old walnut trees along
the wall that I wanted to live forever
would have fallen the stone barns would be empty
the stone basins empty the dormers staring
into distances above dry grass and
the wide valley and I would see my own hand
at the door in the sunlight turn the key
and open to the sky at the empty
windows across the room that would still be there

THE VIXEN

1996

Fox Sleep

On a road through the mountains with a friend many years ago
       I came to a curve on a slope where a clear stream
flowed down flashing across dark rocks through its own
       echoes that could neither be caught nor forgotten
it was the turning of autumn and already
       the mornings were cold with ragged clouds in the hollows
long after sunrise but the pasture sagging like a roof
       the glassy water and flickering yellow leaves
in the few poplars and knotted plum trees were held up
       in a handful of sunlight that made the slates on the silent
mill by the stream glisten white above their ruin
       and a few relics of the life before had been arranged
in front of the open mill house to wait
       pale in the daylight out on the open mountain
after whatever they had been made for was over
       the dew was drying on them and there were few who took that road
who might buy one of them and take it away somewhere
       to be unusual to be the only one
to become unknown a wooden bed stood there on rocks
       a cradle the color of dust a cracked oil jar iron pots
wooden wheels iron wheels stone wheels the tall box of a clock
       and among them a ring of white stone the size of an
embrace set into another of the same size
       an iron spike rising from the ring where the wooden
handle had fitted that turned it in its days as a hand mill
       you could see if you looked closely that the top ring
that turned in the other had been carved long before in the form
       of a fox lying nose in tail seeming to be
asleep the features worn almost away where it
       had gone around and around grinding grain and salt
to go into the dark and to go on and remember

What I thought I had left I kept finding again
        but when I went looking for what I thought I remembered
as anyone could have foretold it was not there
        when I went away looking for what I had to do
I found that I was living where I was a stranger
        but when I retraced my steps the familiar vision
turned opaque and all surface and in the wrong places
        and the places where I had been a stranger appeared to me
to be where I had been at home called by name and answering
        getting ready to go away and going away

Every time they assembled and he spoke to them
        about waking there was an old man who stood listening
and left before the others until one day the old man stayed
        and Who are you he asked the old man
and the old man answered I am not a man
        many lives ago I stood where you are standing
and they assembled in front of me and I spoke to them
        about waking until one day one of them asked me
When someone has wakened to what is really there
        is that person free of the chain of consequences
and I answered yes and with that I turned into a fox
        and I have been a fox for five hundred lives
and now I have come to ask you to say what will
        free me from the body of a fox please tell me
when someone has wakened to what is really there
        is that person free of the chain of consequences
and this time the answer was That person sees it as it is
        then the old man said Thank you for waking me

you have set me free of the body of the fox
　　　which you will find on the other side of the mountain
I ask you to bury it please as one of your own
　　　that evening he announced a funeral service
for one of them but they said nobody has died
　　　then he led them to the other side of the mountain
and a cave where they found a fox's body
　　　and he told them the story and they buried the fox
as one of them but later one of them asked
　　　what if he had given the right answer every time

　　　　　　　*

Once again I was there and once again I was leaving
　　　and again it seemed as though nothing had changed
even while it was all changing but this time
　　　was a time of ending this time the long marriage was over
the orbits were flying apart it was autumn again
　　　sunlight tawny in the fields where the shadows
each day grew longer and the still afternoons
　　　ripened the distance until the sun went down
across the valley and the full moon rose out of the trees
　　　it was the time of year when I was born and that evening
I went to see friends for the last time and I came back
　　　after midnight along the road white with the moon
I was crossing the bars of shadow and seeing ahead of me
　　　the wide silent valley full of silver light
and there just at the corner of the land that I had
　　　come back to so many times and now was leaving
at the foot of the wall built of pale stone I saw the body
　　　stretched in the grass and it was a fox a vixen
just dead with no sign of how it had come to happen
　　　no blood the long fur warm in the dewy grass

nothing broken or lost or torn or unfinished
      I carried her home to bury her in the garden
in the morning of the clear autumn that she had left
      and to stand afterward in the turning daylight

         *

There are the yellow beads of the stonecrops and the twisted flags
      of dried irises knuckled into the hollows
of moss and rubbly limestone on the waves of the low wall
      the ivy has climbed along them where the weasel ran
the light has kindled to gold the late leaves of the cherry tree
      over the lane by the house chimney there is the roof
and the window looking out over the garden
      summer and winter there is the field below the house
there is the broad valley far below them all with the curves
      of the river a strand of sky threaded through it
and the notes of bells rising out of it faint as smoke
      and there beyond the valley above the rim of the wall
the line of mountains I recognize like a line of writing
      that has come back when I had thought it was forgotten

Threshold

Swallows streaking in and out through the row of broken
      panes over the front door went on with their conversation
of afterthoughts whatever they had been settling
      about early summer and nests and the late daylight
and the vacant dwellings of swallows in the beams
      let their dust filter down as I brought in my bed
while the door stood open onto the stone sill smoothed to water
      by the feet of inhabitants never known to me
and when I turned to look back I did not recognize a thing
      the sound of flying whirred past me a voice called far away
the swallows grew still and bats came out light as breath
      around the stranger by himself in the echoes
what did I have to do with anything I could remember
      all I did not know went on beginning around me
I had thought it would come later but it had been waiting

White Morning

On nights toward the end of summer an age of mist
      has gathered in the oaks the box thickets the straggling
eglantines it has moved like a hand unable to believe
      the face it touches over the velvet of wild thyme
and the vetches sinking with the weight of dew it has found
      its way without sight into the hoofprints of cows
the dark nests long empty the bark hanging along the narrow
      halls among stones and has held it all in a cloud
unseen the whole night as in a mind where I came
      when it was turning white and I was holding a thin
wet branch wrapped in lichens because all I had thought
      I knew had to be passed from branch to branch through the empty
sky and whatever I reached then and could recognize
      moved toward me out of the cloud and was still the sky
where I went on looking until I was standing on
      the wide wall along the lane to the hazel grove
where we went one day to cut handles that would last
      the crows were calling around me to white air
I could hear their wings dripping and hear small birds with lights
      breaking in their tongues the cold soaked through me I was able
after that morning to believe stories that once
      would have been closed to me I saw a carriage go under
the oaks there in full day and vanish I watched animals there
      I sat with friends in the shade they have all disappeared
most of the stories have to do with vanishing

François de Maynard 1582–1646

When I cannot see my angel I would rather
      have been born blind and miserable I wrote at one time
then the season of flowers I said appeared to be
      painted black and it was impossible through those days
to imagine how I could have tarried so long
      on the earth while the syllables of thirty Aprils
had dripped like ice in the mountains and I had listened
      to the water as a song I might know and now
the autumn is almost done and the days arrive each one
      expecting less how long it is since I left
the court I loved once the passions there the skins of morning
      the colors of vain May and my hopes always for something
else that would be the same but more and never failing
      more praise more laurels more loves more bounty until I
could believe I was Ronsard and I wrote that I would have
      a monument as for a demigod whatever
that might be when I will be lucky to be buried
      as the poor are buried without noise and the faces covered
and be gone as the year goes out and be honored as a blank wall
      in a cold chapel of the church where I shivered as a child
beside my father the judge in his complete black those years when
      soldiers clattered and clanged through the streets horsemen clashed
under the windows and the nights rang with the screams
      of the wounded outside the walls while the farms burned
into dawns red with smoke and blood came spreading
      through the canals at the foot of those towers on the hill
that I would see again and again after every absence
      fingers of a hand rising out of the gray valley
in the distance and coming closer to become here as before
      where my mother wanted me where I married

where the banquets glittered along the river to my songs
        where my daughter died and how cold the house turned all at once
I have seen the waves of war come back and break over us here
        I have smelled rosemary and juniper burning in the plague
I have gone away and away I have held a post in Rome
        I have caught my death there I have flattered evil men
and gained nothing by it I have sat beside my wife
        when she could move no longer I sat here beside her
I watched the gold leaves of the poplars floating on the stream
        long ago the gold current of the river Pactolus
was compared to eternity but the poplar leaves have gone
        in the years when I rode to Aurillac I used to stop
at a place where the mountains appeared to open before me
        and turning I could still see all the way back to here
and both ways were my life which now I have slept through to wake
        in a dark house talking to the shadows about love

Hölderlin at the River

The ice again in my sleep it was following someone
    it thought was me in the dark and I recognized its white tongue
it held me in its freezing radiance until I
    was the only tree there and I broke and carried
my limbs down through dark rocks calling to the summer
    where are you where will you be how could I have missed you
gold skin the still pond shining under the eglantines
    warm peach resting in my palm at noon among flowers
all the way I was looking for you and I had nothing to say who I was
    until the last day of the world then far below I could see
the great valley as night fell the one ray withdrawing
    like the note of a horn and afterwards black wind took
all I knew but here is the foreign morning with its clouds
    sailing on water beyond the black trembling poplars
the sky breathless around its blinding fire and the white flocks
    in water meadows on the far shore are flowing past their
silent shepherds and now only once I hear the hammer
    ring on the anvil and in some place that I have not seen
a bird of ice is singing of its own country
    if any of this remains it will not be me

One of the Lives

If I had not met the red-haired boy whose father
      had broken a leg parachuting into Provence
to join the resistance in the final stage of the war
      and so had been killed there as the Germans were moving north
out of Italy and if the friend who was with him
      as he was dying had not had an elder brother
who also died young quite differently in peacetime
      leaving two children one of them with bad health
who had been kept out of school for a whole year by an illness
      and if I had written anything else at the top
of the examination form where it said college
      of your choice or if the questions that day had been
put differently and if a young woman in Kittanning
      had not taught my father to drive at the age of twenty
so that he got the job with the pastor of the big church
      in Pittsburgh where my mother was working and if
my mother had not lost both parents when she was a child
      so that she had to go to her grandmother's in Pittsburgh
I would not have found myself on an iron cot
      with my head by the fireplace of a stone farmhouse
that had stood empty since some time before I was born
      I would not have travelled so far to lie shivering
with fever though I was wrapped in everything in the house
      nor have watched the unctuous doctor hold up his needle
at the window in the rain light of October
      I would not have seen through the cracked pane the darkening
valley with its river sliding past the amber mountains
      nor have wakened hearing plums fall in the small hour
thinking I knew where I was as I heard them fall

Vixen

Comet of stillness princess of what is over
    high note held without trembling without voice without sound
aura of complete darkness keeper of the kept secrets
    of the destroyed stories the escaped dreams the sentences
never caught in words warden of where the river went
    touch of its surface sibyl of the extinguished
window onto the hidden place and the other time
    at the foot of the wall by the road patient without waiting
in the full moonlight of autumn at the hour when I was born
    you no longer go out like a flame at the sight of me
you are still warmer than the moonlight gleaming on you
    even now you are unharmed even now perfect
as you have always been now when your light paws are running
    on the breathless night on the bridge with one end I remember you
when I have heard you the soles of my feet have made answer
    when I have seen you I have waked and slipped from the calendars
from the creeds of difference and the contradictions
    that were my life and all the crumbling fabrications
as long as it lasted until something that we were
    had ended when you are no longer anything
let me catch sight of you again going over the wall
    and before the garden is extinct and the woods are figures
guttering on a screen let my words find their own
    places in the silence after the animals

A Given Day

When I wake I find it is late in the autumn
      the hard rain has passed and the sunlight has not yet reached
the tips of the dark leaves that are their own shadows still
      and I am home it is coming back to me I am
remembering the gradual sweetness of morning
      the clear spring of being here as it rises one by one
in silence and without a pause and is the only one
      then one at a time I remember without understanding
some that have gone and arise only not to be here
      an afternoon walking on a bridge thinking of a friend
when she was still alive while a door from a building
      being demolished sailed down through the passing city
my mother half my age at a window long since removed
      friends in the same rooms and the words dreaming between us
the eyes of animals upon me they are all here
      in the clearness of the morning in the first light
that remembers its way now to the flowers of winter

THE FOLDING CLIFFS: A NARRATIVE

1998

The Cliffs

36.

The next day they were down there and they heard voices again
        and watched from hiding and saw Kelau and his wife
Keapoulu coming down the same trail and they went out
        and greeted each other in the old way this time
without suspicion crying and embracing each other
        and their friends had brought along clothes for all of them
and matches and a bag of fish caught that night and another
        of dried fish and some cooking pots and knives and gourds
and they cried together and ate together talking
        about friends they all knew and what had happened to each one
since the summer and Kelau and Keapoulu
        sat with them through the middle of the day talking
they were all trying to tell each other everything
        Kelau said that a few people of Kalalau
were talking about moving back and rebuilding their houses
        and Koʻolau nodded and said—You will remember
not to tell anyone that you have seen us here—and they
        promised and promised again as they were saying good-bye
and after they were gone months passed and became years
        in which they spoke with no one else though they saw people
they knew come back into the valley Wahinealoha
        came back with his wife and they built their house again
in the old place and cleaned out their taro ponds and they kept
        chickens a few at first and then there were many of them
and Piʻilani or Koʻolau went every day
        and watched what they were doing but Koʻolau said
that Wahinealoha should not know that they were there
        He said—He is someone who says yes to everybody—

and they agreed that they must let no one in the valley
           know that they were there because then everyone would know
and Kelau had said he had heard that a reward
           had been offered to whoever could catch Koʻolau
so they moved more often than before taking more care
           to leave nothing behind them that would show that they had
                   been there
they watched the Pā family come back and build their house again
           and then one neighbor after another but they never
showed themselves and they saw cattle from time to time
           that must have been Wili Kini's and Koʻolau's rifle
was never far but he said he would not use it again
           except to protect them and Kaleimanu grew weaker
month by month and his nose shrank away and his mouth puckered
           it was hard for him to hold anything and he shivered
more often and for longer and they carried him everywhere

THE RIVER SOUND

1999

The Stranger

after a Guarani legend recorded by
Ernesto Morales

One day in the forest there was somebody
who had never been there before
it was somebody like the monkeys but taller
and without a tail and without so much hair
standing up and walking on only two feet
and as he went he heard a voice calling Save me

as the stranger looked he could see a snake
a very big snake with a circle of fire
that was dancing all around it
and the snake was trying to get out
but every way it turned the fire was there

so the stranger bent the trunk of a young tree
and climbed out over the fire until he
could hold a branch down to the snake
and the snake wrapped himself around the branch
and the stranger pulled the snake up out of the fire

and as soon as the snake saw that he was free
he twined himself around the stranger
and started to crush the life out of him
but the stranger shouted No No
I am the one who has just saved your life
and you pay me back by trying to kill me

but the snake said I am keeping the law
it is the law that whoever does good

receives evil in return
and he drew his coils tight around the stranger
but the stranger kept on saying No No
I do not believe that is the law

so the snake said I will show you
I will show you three times and you will see
and he kept his coils tight around the stranger's neck
and all around his arms and body
but he let go of the stranger's legs
Now walk he said to the stranger Keep going

so they started out that way and they came
to a river and the river said to them
I do good to everyone and look what they
do to me I save them from dying of thirst
and all they do is stir up the mud
and fill my water with dead things

the snake said One

the stranger said Let us go on and they did
and they came to a carandá-i palm
there were wounds running with sap on its trunk
and the palm tree was moaning I do good
to everyone and look what they do to me
I give them my fruit and my shade and they cut me
and drink from my body until I die

the snake said Two

the stranger said Let us go on and they did
and came to a place where they heard whimpering
and saw a dog with his paw in a basket
and the dog said I did a good thing

and this is what came of it
I found a jaguar who had been hurt
and I took care of him and he got better

and as soon as he had his strength again
he sprang at me wanting to eat me up
I managed to get away but he tore my paw
I hid in a cave until he was gone
and here in this basket I have
a calabash full of milk for my wound
but now I have pushed it too far down to reach

will you help me he said to the snake
and the snake liked milk better than anything
so he slid off the stranger and into the basket
and when he was inside the dog snapped it shut
and swung it against a tree with all his might
again and again until the snake was dead

and after the snake was dead in there
the dog said to the stranger Friend
I have saved your life
and the stranger took the dog home with him
and treated him the way the stranger would treat a dog

The Chinese Mountain Fox

Now we can tell that there
must once have been a time
when it was always there
and might at any time

appear out of nowhere
as they were wont to say
and probably to their
age it did look that way

though how are we to say
from the less than certain
evidence of our day
and they referred often

through the centuries when
it may have been a sight
they considered common
so that they mentioned it

as a presence they were
sure everyone had seen
and would think familiar
they alluded even

then until it became
their unquestioned habit
like a part of the name
to that element it

had of complete surprise
of being suddenly

the blaze in widened eyes
that had been turned only

at that moment upon
some place quite near that they
all through their lives had known
and passed by every day

perhaps at the same place
where they themselves had just
been standing that live face
looking as though it must

have been following them
would have appeared with no
warning they could fathom
or ever come to know

though they made studied use
of whatever system
logic calculus ruse
they trusted in their time

to tell them where they might
count on it next and when
if once they figured right
as though it travelled in

a pattern they could track
like the route of some far
light in the zodiac
comet or migrant star

but it was never where
they had thought it would be

and showed the best of their
beliefs successively

to be without substance
shadows they used to cast
old tales and illusions
out of some wishful past

each in turn was consigned
to the role of legend
while yet another kind
of legend had wakened

to play the animal
even while it was there
the unpredictable
still untaken creature

part lightning and part rust
the fiction was passed down
with undiminished trust
while the sightings began

to be unusual
secondhand dubious
unverifiable
turning to ghost stories

all the more easily
since when it had been seen
most times that was only
by someone all alone

and unlike its cousins
of the lowlands captive

all these generations
and kept that way alive

never had it been caught
poisoned or hunted down
by packs of dogs or shot
hung up mounted or worn

never even been seen
twice by the same person
in the place it had been
when they looked there again

and whatever they told
of it as long as they
still spoke of it revealed
always more of the way

they looked upon the light
while it was theirs to see
and what they thought it might
let them glimpse at any

moment than of the life
that they had rarely been
able to catch sight of
in an instant between

now and where it had been
at large before they came
when the mountains were green
before it had a name

Lament for the Makers

I that all through my early days
I remember well was always
    the youngest of the company
    save for one sister after me

from the time when I was able
to walk under the dinner table
    and be punished for that promptly
    because its leaves could fall on me

father and mother overhead
who they talked with and what they said
    were mostly clouds that knew already
    directions far too old for me

at school I skipped a grade so that
whatever I did after that
    each year everyone would be
    older and hold it up to me

at college many of my friends
were returning veterans
    equipped with an authority
    I admired and they treated me

as the kid some years below them
so I married half to show them
    and listened with new vanity
    when I heard it said of me

how young I was and what a shock
I was the youngest on the block
　　I thought I had it coming to me
　　and I believe it mattered to me

and seemed my own and there to stay
for a while then came the day
　　I was in another country
　　other older friends around me

my youth by then taken for granted
and found that it had been supplanted
　　the notes in some anthology
　　listed persons born after me

how long had that been going on
how could I be not quite so young
　　and not notice and nobody
　　even bother to inform me

though my fond hopes were taking longer
than I had hoped when I was younger
　　a phrase that came more frequently
　　to suggest itself to me

but the secret was still there
safe in the unprotected air
　　that breath that in its own words only
　　sang when I was a child to me

and caught me helpless to convey it
with nothing but the words to say it
　　though it was those words completely
　　and they rang it was clear to me

with a changeless overtone
I have listened for since then
      hearing that note endlessly
      vary every time beyond me

trying to find where it comes from
and to what words it may come
      and forever after be
      present for the thought kept at me

that my mother and every day
of our lives would slip away
      like the summer and suddenly
      all would have been taken from me

but that presence I had known
sometimes in words would not be gone
      and if it spoke even once for me
      it would stay there and be me

however few might choose those words
for listening to afterwards
      there I would be awake to see
      a world that looked unchanged to me

I suppose that was what I thought
young as I was then and that note
      sang from the words of somebody
      in my twenties I looked around me

to all the poets who were then
living and whose lines had been
      sustenance and company
      and a light for years to me

I found the portraits of their faces
first in the rows of oval spaces
        in Oscar Williams' *Treasury*
        so they were settled long before me

and they would always be the same
in that distance of their fame
        affixed in immortality
        during their lifetimes while around me

all was woods seen from a train
no sooner glimpsed than gone again
        but those immortals constantly
        in some measure reassured me

then first there was Dylan Thomas
from the White Horse taken from us
        to the brick wall I woke to see
        for years across the street from me

then word of the death of Stevens
brought a new knowledge of silence
        the nothing not there finally
        the sparrow saying Bethou me

how long his long auroras had
played on the darkness overhead
        since I looked up from my Shelley
        and Arrowsmith first showed him to me

and not long from his death until
Edwin Muir had fallen still
        that fine bell of the latter day
        not well heard yet it seems to me

Sylvia Plath then took her own
direction into the unknown
from her last stars and poetry
in the house a few blocks from me

Williams a little afterwards
was carried off by the black rapids
that flowed through Paterson as he
said and their rushing sound is in me

that was the time that gathered Frost
into the dark where he was lost
to us but from too far to see
his voice keeps coming back to me

then the sudden news that Ted
Roethke had been found floating dead
in someone's pool at night but he
still rises from his lines for me

MacNeice watched the cold light harden
when that day had left the garden
stepped into the dark ground to see
where it went but never told me

and on the rimless wheel in turn
Eliot spun and Jarrell was borne
off by a car who had loved to see
the racetrack then there came to me

one day the knocking at the garden
door and the news that Berryman
from the bridge had leapt who twenty
years before had quoted to me

the passage where *a jest* wrote Crane
falls from the speechless caravan
        with a wave to Bones and Henry
        and to all that he had told me

I dreamed that Auden sat up in bed
but I could not catch what he said
        by that time he was already
        dead someone next morning told me

and Marianne Moore entered the ark
Pound would say no more from the dark
        who once had helped to set me free
        I thought of the prose around me

and David Jones would rest until
the turn of time under the hill
        but from the sleep of Arthur he
        wakes an echo that follows me

Lowell thought the shadow skyline
coming toward him was Manhattan
        but it blacked out in the taxi
        once he read his *Notebook* to me

at the number he had uttered
to the driver a last word
        then that watchful and most lonely
        wanderer whose words went with me

everywhere Elizabeth
Bishop lay alone in death
        they were leaving the party early
        our elders it came home to me

but the needle moved among us
taking always by surprise
              flicking by too fast to see
              to touch a friend born after me

and James Wright by his darkened river
heard the night heron pass over
              took his candle down the frosty
              road and disappeared before me

Howard Moss had felt the gnawing
at his name and found that nothing
              made it better he was funny
              even so about it to me

Graves in his nineties lost the score
forgot that he had died before
              found his way back innocently
              who once had been a guide to me

Nemerov sadder than his verse
said a new year could not be worse
              then the black flukes of agony
              went down leaving the words with me

Stafford watched his hand catch the light
seeing that it was time to write
              a memento of their story
              signed and is a plain before me

now Jimmy Merrill's voice is heard
like an aria afterward
              and we know he will never be
              old after all who spoke to me

on the cold street that last evening
of his heart that leapt at finding
        some yet unknown poetry
        then waved through the window to me

in that city we were born in
one by one they have all gone
        out of the time and language we
        had in common which have brought me

to this season after them
the best words did not keep them from
        leaving themselves finally
        as this day is going from me

and the clear note they were hearing
never promised anything
        but the true sound of brevity
        that will go on after me

The Wren

Paper clips are rusted to the pages
before I have come back to hear a bell
I recognize out of another age
echo from the cold mist of one morning
in white May and then a wren still singing
from the thicket at the foot of the wall

that is one of the voices without question
and without answer like the beam of some
star familiar but in no sense known threading
time upon time on its solitary way
once more I hear it without understanding
and without division in the new day

This Time

Many things I seem to have done backward
as a child I wanted to be older
now I am trying to remember why
and what it was like to have to pretend
day after day I saw places that I
did not recognize until later on
when nothing was left of them any more
there were meetings and partings that passed me
at the time like train windows with the days
slipping across them and long afterward
the moment and sense of them came to me
burning there were faces I knew for years
and the nearness of them began only
when they were missing and there were seasons
of anguish I recalled with affection
joys lost unnoticed and searched for later
with no sign to show where they had last been
there with me and there was love which is thought
to be a thing of youth and I found it
I was sure that was what it was as I
came to it again and again sometimes
without knowing it sometimes insisting
vainly upon the name but I came to
the best of it last and though it may be
shorter this way I am glad it is so
it would have been too brief at any time
and so much of what I had found early
had been lost as I made my way to this
which is what I was to know afterward

THE PUPIL

2001

Prophecy

At the end of the year the stars go out
the air stops breathing and the Sibyl sings
first she sings of the darkness she can see
she sings on until she comes to the age
without time and the dark she cannot see

no one hears then as she goes on singing
of all the white days that were brought to us one
by one that turned to colors around us

a light coming from far out in the eye
where it begins before she can see it

burns through the words that no one has believed

Sonnet

Where it begins will remain a question
for the time being at least which is to
say for this lifetime and there is no
other life that can be this one again
and where it goes after that only one
at a time is ever about to know
though we have it by heart as one and though
we remind each other on occasion

How often may the clarinet rehearse
alone the one solo before the one
time that is heard after all the others
telling the one thing that they all tell of
it is the sole performance of a life
come back I say to it over the waters

In the Open

Those summer nights when the planes came over
it seemed it was every night that summer
after the still days of perfect weather
I kept telling myself what it was not
that I was feeling as the afternoon
light deepened into the lingering
radiance that colored its leaving us
that was the light through which I would come home
again and again with the day over
picking my way from Whitehall through the new
rubble in the known streets the broken glass
signalling from among the crevices
fallen facades hoses among the mounds
figures in rubber coming and going
at the ruins or gathered with lowered
voices they all spoke in lowered voices
as I recall now so that all I heard
was the murmured current I can still hear
how many in that building I might hear
something like that how many in that one
then a quiet street the shop doors open
figures waiting in lines without a word
with the night ahead no it was not fear
I said to myself that was not the word
for whatever I heard as the door closed
as we talked of the day as we listened
as the fork touched the plate like a greeting
as the curtains were drawn as the cat stretched
as the news came on with word of losses
warning of the night as we picked up the ground sheet
and the folded blankets as I bent down

to remember the fur of Tim the cat
as the door closed and the stairs in the dark
led us back down to the street and the night
swung wide before us once more in the park

Often after the all-clear it would be
very cold suddenly a reminder
hardly more than that as I understood
of the great cold of the dark everywhere
around us deeper than I could believe
usually she was asleep by then
warm and breathing softly I could picture
how she must look the long curve of her lips
the high white forehead I wondered about
her eyelids and what calm they had come to
while the ice reached me much of the night was
in pieces by then behind me piled up
like rubble all fallen into the same
disorder the guns shouting from the hill
the drones and the broad roar of planes the screams
of sirens the pumping of bombs coming
closer the beams groping over the smoke
they all seemed to have ended somewhere without
saying this is the last one you seldom
hear the dog stop barking there were people
on all sides of us in the park asleep
awake the sky was clear I lay looking
up into it through the cold to the lights
the white moments that had travelled so long
each one of them to become visible
to us then only for that time and then
where did they go in the dark afterward
the invisible dark the cold never
felt or ever to be felt where was it

then as I lay looking up into all
that had been coming to pass and was still
coming to pass some of the stars by then
were nothing but the light that had left them
before there was life on earth and nothing
would be seen after them and the light from
one of them would have set out exactly
when the first stir of life recognized death
and began its delays that light had been
on its way from there all through what happened
afterward through the beginning of pain
the return of pain into the senses
into feelings without words and then words
travelling toward us even in our sleep
words for the feelings of those who are not
there now and words we say are for ourselves
then sounds of feet went by in the damp grass
dark figures slipping away toward morning

Home Tundra

It may be that the hour is snow
seeming never to settle not
even to be cold now slipping
away from underneath into
the past from which no sounds follow
what I hear is the dogs breathing
ahead of me in the shadow

two of them have already gone
far on into the dark of closed
pages out of sight and hearing
two of them are old already
one cannot hear one cannot see

even in sleep they are running
drawing me with them on their way
wrapped in a day I found today
we know where we are because we
are together here together
leaving no footprints in the hour

whatever the diaries say
nobody ever found the pole

PRESENT COMPANY

2005

To the Face in the Mirror

Because you keep turning toward me
what I suppose must be
my own features only
backward it seems to me
that you are able to see
me only by
looking back from somewhere
that is a picture of here
at this moment but
reversed and already
not anywhere

so how far
away are you
after all who seem to be
so near and eternally
out of reach
you with the white hair
now who still surprise me
day after day
staring back at me
out of nowhere
past present or future
you with no weight or name
no will of your own
and the sight of me
shining in your eye

how do you
know it is me

To the Margin

Following the black
footprints the tracks
of words that have passed that way
before me I come
again and again to
your blank shore

not the end yet
but there is nothing more
to be seen there
to be read to be followed
to be understood
and each time I turn
back to go on
in the same way
that I draw the next breath

the wider you are
the emptier and the more
innocent of any
signal the more
precious the text
feels to me as I make
my way through it reminding
myself listening
for any sound from you

To the Words

When it happens you are not there

O you beyond numbers
beyond recollection
passed on from breath to breath
given again
from day to day from age
to age
charged with knowledge
knowing nothing

indifferent elders
indispensable and sleepless

keepers of our names
before ever we came
to be called by them

you that were
formed to begin with
you that were cried out
you that were spoken
to begin with
to say what could not be said

ancient precious
and helpless ones

say it

September 17, 2001

To the Book

Go on then
in your own time
this is as far
as I will take you
I am leaving your words with you
as though they had been yours
all the time

of course you are not finished
how can you be finished
when the morning begins again
or the moon rises
even the words are not finished
though they may claim to be

never mind
I will not be
listening when they say
how you should be
different in some way
you will be able to tell them
that the fault was all mine

whoever I was
when I made you up

THE SHADOW OF SIRIUS

2008

The Nomad Flute

You that sang to me once sing to me now
let me hear your long lifted note
survive with me
the star is fading
I can think farther than that but I forget
do you hear me

do you still hear me
does your air
remember you
o breath of morning
night song morning song
I have with me
all that I do not know
I have lost none of it

but I know better now
than to ask you
where you learned that music
where any of it came from
once there were lions in China

I will listen until the flute stops
and the light is old again

Still Morning

It appears now that there is only one
age and it knows
nothing of age as the flying birds know
nothing of the air they are flying through
or of the day that bears them up
through themselves
and I am a child before there are words
arms are holding me up in a shadow
voices murmur in a shadow
as I watch one patch of sunlight moving
across the green carpet
in a building
gone long ago and all the voices
silent and each word they said in that time
silent now
while I go on seeing that patch of sunlight

Note

Remember how the naked soul
comes to language and at once knows
loss and distance and believing

then for a time it will not run
with its old freedom
like a light innocent of measure
but will hearken to how
one story becomes another
and will try to tell where
they have emerged from
and where they are heading
as though they were its own legend
running before the words and beyond them
naked and never looking back

through the noise of questions

From the Start

Who did I think was listening
when I wrote down the words
in pencil at the beginning
words for singing
to music I did not know
and people I did not know
would read them and stand to sing them
already knowing them
while they sing they have no names

Far Along in the Story

The boy walked on with a flock of cranes
following him calling as they came
from the horizon behind him
sometimes he thought he could recognize
a voice in all that calling but he
could not hear what they were calling
and when he looked back he could not tell
one of them from another in their
rising and falling but he went on
trying to remember something in
their calls until he stumbled and came
to himself with the day before him
wide open and the stones of the path
lying still and each tree in its own leaves
the cranes were gone from the sky and at
that moment he remembered who he was
only he had forgotten his name

Youth

Through all of youth I was looking for you
without knowing what I was looking for

or what to call you I think I did not
even know I was looking how would I

have known you when I saw you as I did
time after time when you appeared to me

as you did naked offering yourself
entirely at that moment and you let

me breathe you touch you taste you knowing
no more than I did and only when I

began to think of losing you did I
recognize you when you were already

part memory part distance remaining
mine in the ways that I learn to miss you

from what we cannot hold the stars are made

Little Soul

after Hadrian

Little soul little stray
little drifter
now where will you stay
all pale and all alone
after the way
you used to make fun of things

Going

Only humans believe
there is a word for goodbye
we have one in every language
one of the first words we learn
it is made out of greeting
but they are going away
the raised hand waving
the face the person the place
the animal the day
leaving the word behind
and what it was meant to say

Worn Words

The late poems are the ones
I turn to first now
following a hope that keeps
beckoning me
waiting somewhere in the lines
almost in plain sight

it is the late poems
that are made of words
that have come the whole way
they have been there

A Letter to Su Tung-p'o

Almost a thousand years later
I am asking the same questions
you did the ones you kept finding
yourself returning to as though
nothing had changed except the tone
of their echo growing deeper
and what you knew of the coming
of age before you had grown old
I do not know any more now
than you did then about what you
were asking as I sit at night
above the hushed valley thinking
of you on your river that one
bright sheet of moonlight in the dream
of the waterbirds and I hear
the silence after your questions
how old are the questions tonight

The Long and the Short of It

As long as we can believe anything
we believe in measure
we do it with the first breath we take
and the first sound we make
it is in each word we learn
and in each of them it means
what will come again and when
it is there in *meal* and in *moon*
and in *meaning* it is the meaning
it is the firmament and the furrow
turning at the end of the field
and the verse turning with its breath
it is in memory that keeps telling us
some of the old story about us

To Paula in Late Spring

Let me imagine that we will come again
when we want to and it will be spring
we will be no older than we ever were
the worn griefs will have eased like the early cloud
through which the morning slowly comes to itself
and the ancient defenses against the dead
will be done with and left to the dead at last
the light will be as it is now in the garden
that we have made here these years together
of our long evenings and astonishment

Nocturne II

August arrives in the dark

we are not even asleep and it is here
with a gust of rain rustling before it
how can it be so late all at once
somewhere the Perseids are falling
toward us already at a speed that would
burn us alive if we could believe it
but in the stillness after the rain ends
nothing is to be heard but the drops falling
one at a time from the tips of the leaves
into the night and I lie in the dark
listening to what I remember
while the night flies on with us into itself

Rain Light

All day the stars watch from long ago
my mother said I am going now
when you are alone you will be all right
whether or not you know you will know
look at the old house in the dawn rain
all the flowers are forms of water
the sun reminds them through a white cloud
touches the patchwork spread on the hill
the washed colors of the afterlife
that lived there long before you were born
see how they wake without a question
even though the whole world is burning

The Laughing Thrush

O nameless joy of the morning

tumbling upward note by note out of the night
and the hush of the dark valley
and out of whatever has not been there

song unquestioning and unbounded
yes this is the place and the one time
in the whole of before and after
with all of memory waking into it

and the lost visages that hover
around the edge of sleep
constant and clear
and the words that lately have fallen silent
to surface among the phrases of some future
if there is a future

here is where they all sing the first daylight
whether or not there is anyone listening

THE MOON BEFORE MORNING

2014

Homecoming

Once only when the summer
was nearly over and my own
hair had been white as the day's clouds
for more years than I was counting
I looked across the garden at evening
Paula was still weeding around
flowers that open after dark
and I looked up to the clear sky
and saw the new moon and at that
moment from behind me a band
of dark birds and then another
after it flying in silence
long curving wings hardly moving
the plovers just in from the sea
and the flight clear from Alaska
half their weight gone to get them home
but home now arriving without
a sound as it rose to meet them

Dew Light

Now in the blessed days of more and less
when the news about time is that each day
there is less of it I know none of that
as I walk out through the early garden
only the day and I are here with no
before or after and the dew looks up
without a number or a present age

Beginners

As though it had always been forbidden to remember
each of us grew up
knowing nothing about the beginning

but in time there came from that forgetting
names representing a truth of their own
and we went on repeating them
until they too began not to be remembered
they became part of the forgetting
later came stories like the days themselves
there seemed to be no end to them
and we told what we could remember of them

though we always forgot where they came from
and forgot that it was forbidden
and whether it had been forbidden
but from forgotten pain we recognize
sometimes the truth when it is told to us
and from forgotten happiness we know
that the day we wake to is our own

Antique Sound

There was an age when you played records
with ordinary steel needles which grew blunt
and damaged the grooves or with more expensive
stylus tips said to be tungsten or diamond
which wore down the records and the music receded
but a friend and I had it on persuasive authority
that the best thing was a dry thorn of the right kind
and I knew where to find those off to the left
of the Kingston Pike in the shallow swale
that once had been forest and had grown back
into a scrubby wilderness alive with
an earthly choir of crickets blackbirds finches
crows jays the breathing of voles raccoons
rabbits foxes the breeze in the thickets
the thornbushes humming a high polyphony
all long gone since to improvement but while
that fine dissonance was in tune we rode out
on bicycles to break off dry thorn branches
picking the thorns and we took back the harvest
and listened to Beethoven's Rassoumoffsky
quartets echoed from the end of a thorn

Wild Oats

Watching the first sunlight
touch the tops of the palms
what could I ask

All the beads have gone
from the old string
and the string does not miss them

The daughters of memory
never pronounce
their own names

In the language of heaven
the angel said
go make your own garden

I dream I am here
in the morning
and the dream is its own time

Looking into the old well
I see my own face
then another behind it

There I am
morning clouds
in the east wind

No one is in the garden
the autumn daisies
have the day to themselves

All night in the dark valley
the sound of rain arriving
from another time

September when the wind
drops and to us it seems
that the days are waiting

I needed my mistakes
in their own order
to get me here

Here is the full moon
bringing us
silence

I call that singing bird my friend
though I know nothing else about him
and he does not know I exist

What is it that I keep forgetting
now I have lost it again
right here

I have to keep telling myself
why I am going away again
I do not seem to listen

In my youth I believed in somewhere else
I put faith in travel
now I am becoming my own tree

How It Happens

The sky said I am watching
to see what you
can make out of nothing
I was looking up and I said
I thought you
were supposed to be doing that
the sky said Many
are clinging to that
I am giving you a chance
I was looking up and I said
I am the only chance I have
then the sky did not answer
and here we are
with our names for the days
the vast days that do not listen to us

Convenience

We were not made in its image
but from the beginning we believed in it
not for the pure appeasement of hunger
but for its availability
it could command our devotion
beyond question and without our consent
and by whatever name we have called it
in its name love has been set aside
unmeasured time has been devoted to it
forests have been erased and rivers poisoned
and truth has been relegated for it
wars have been sanctified by it
we believe that we have a right to it
even though it belongs to no one
we carry a way back to it everywhere
we are sure that it is saving something
we consider it our personal savior
all we have to pay for it is ourselves

Unknown Soldier

Facing us under the helmet
a moment before he is killed
he is a child with a question

Lear's Wife

If he had ever asked me
I could have told him

if he had listened to me
it would have been
another story

I knew them before
they were born

with Goneril at my breast
I looked at the world
and saw blood in darkness
and tried to wake

with Regan at my breast
I looked at the world
and covered my mouth

with Cordelia in my arms
at my breast
I wanted to call out to her
in love and helplessness
and I wept

as for him
he had forgotten me
even before they did

only Cordelia
did not forget
anything

but when asked she said
nothing

Variation on a Theme

Thank you my lifelong afternoon
late in this season of no age
thank you for my windows above the rivers
thank you for the true love you brought me to
when it was time at last and for words
that come out of silence and take me by surprise
and have carried me through the clear day
without once turning to look at me
thank you for friends and long echoes of them
and for those mistakes that were only mine
for the homesickness that guides the young plovers
from somewhere they loved before
they woke into it to another place
they loved before they ever saw it
thank you whole body and hand and eye
thank you for sights and moments known
only to me who will not see them again
except in my mind's eye where they have not changed
thank you for showing me the morning stars
and for the dogs who are guiding me

GARDEN TIME

2016

The Morning

Would I love it this way if it could last
would I love it this way if it
were the whole sky the one heaven
or if I could believe that it belonged to me
a possession that was mine alone
or if I imagined that it noticed me
recognized me and may have come to see me
out of all the mornings that I never knew
and all those that I have forgotten
would I love it this way if I were somewhere else
or if I were younger for the first time
or if these very birds were not singing
or I could not hear them or see their trees
would I love it this way if I were in pain
red torment of body or gray void of grief
would I love it this way if I knew
that I would remember anything that is
here now anything anything

My Other Dark

Sometimes in the dark I find myself
in a place that I seem to have known
in another time
and I wonder
whether it has changed through
sunrises and sunsets that I never saw
whether the things that I remember
are still there where I remember them
would I know them even if my hand
touched them in this present darkness
would they know me and have they been
waiting for me all this time
in the dark

What Can We Call It

It is never what we thought it would be
it was never wished for when it was here
the clouds do not wish for it on their way
the nesting birds are not waiting for it
it is never on time never measured
but it has no promises to keep
it remembers but only for one time
it tells us that it has never left us
but where is it where was it where will it be
where were we where are we where will we be
each time it has taken us by surprise
and vanished before we knew what to say
but who could have taught us what to call it
it can join in our laughter and sometimes
startle us for a moment in our grief
it can be given but can never be sold
it belongs to each one of us alone
yet it is not anyone's possession
wild though it is we fear only its loss

Living with the News

Can I get used to it day after day
a little at a time while the tide keeps
coming in faster the waves get bigger
building on each other breaking records
this is not the world that I remember
then comes the day when I open the box
that I remember packing with such care
and there is the face that I had known well
in little pieces staring up at me
it is not mentioned on the front pages
but somewhere far back near the real estate
among the things that happen every day
to someone who now happens to be me
and what can I do and who can tell me
then there is what the doctor comes to say
endless patience will never be enough
the only hope is to be the daylight

The Wild Geese

It was always for the animals that I grieved most
for the animals I had seen and for those
I had only heard of or dreamed about
or seen in cages or lying beside the road
for those forgotten and those long remembered
for the lost ones that were never found again
among people there were words we all knew
even if we did not say them and although
they were always inadequate when we said them
they were there if we wanted them when the time came
with the animals always there was only
presence as long as it was present and then
only absence suddenly and no word for it
in all the great written wisdom of China
where are the animals when were they lost
where are the ancestors who knew the way
without them all the wise words are bits of sand
twitching on the dunes where the forests
once whispered in their echoing ancient tongue
and the animals knew their way among the trees
only in the old poems does their presence survive
the gibbons call from the mountain gorges
the old words all deepen the great absence
the vastness of all that has been lost
it is still there when the poet in exile
looks up long ago hearing the voices
of wild geese far above him flying home

Here Together

These days I can see us clinging to each other
as we are swept along by the current
I am clinging to you to keep you from
being swept away and you are clinging to me
to keep me from being swept away from you
we see the shores blurring past as we hold
each other in the rushing current
the daylight rushes unheard far above us
how long will we be swept along in the daylight
how long will we cling together in the night
and where will it carry us together

No Believer

Still not believing in age I wake
to find myself older than I can understand
with most of my life in a fragment
that only I remember
some of the old colors are still there
but not the voices or what they are saying
how can it be old when it is now
with the sky taking itself for granted
there was no beginning I was there

Wish

Please one more
kiss in the kitchen
before we turn the lights off

About W. S. Merwin

William Stanley Merwin's dozens of books of poetry, prose, and translation embody experimentation and a sensitivity rooted in environmentalist, pacifist, and anti-imperialist principles. Born in 1927, Merwin "started writing hymns for my father," a Presbyterian minister, "as soon as I could write at all." He attended Princeton University, studying with R.P. Blackmur and his teaching assistant John Berryman. At the age of nineteen, Merwin initiated a nearly twenty-year friendship with Ezra Pound, whose earliest advice to him emphasized "translation [as] a way of keeping one close to what one is doing, to the possibilities of one's own language." After a postgraduate year studying Romance languages, Merwin traveled through Europe, working as a tutor for the Portuguese royal family before settling for a while in Mallorca to tutor Robert Graves's son.

W.H. Auden selected Merwin's first collection, *A Mask for Janus* (1952), for the Yale Series of Younger Poets. Lyrical and ornate, with classical and mythological imagery, the collection registers the influence of Graves and of the medieval poems Merwin was translating.

Merwin's sixth and seventh volumes, *The Lice* (1967) and *The Carrier of Ladders* (1970), address with apocalyptic fervor political corruption and environmental and personal loss. Openly opposed to the Vietnam War, Merwin donated the prize money from his first Pulitzer, for *The Carrier of Ladders,* to antiwar causes. On the dark and mournful tones of this period of the poet's work, he remarks, "Absolute despair has no art, and I imagine the writing of a poem, in whatever mode, still betrays the existence of hope."

To study with the Zen Buddhist master Robert Aitken, Merwin moved to Hawaii, where, in 1983, he married Paula Dunaway Schwartz. Their home in Maui is on a former pineapple plantation whose land they rehabilitated with endangered palm trees. Celebrating Merwin's appointment as United States Poet Laureate in 2010, the *New York Times* declared that he "gives a quiet weight to every word he touches and to the things these words name."

Merwin's poetry continues to attract new readers, and he remains a role model for the artist in times of political turmoil: "We try to save what is passing, if only by describing it, telling it, knowing all the time that we can't do any of these things. The urge to tell it, and the knowledge of the impossibility. Isn't that one reason we write?"

AWARDS AND HONORS

Harold Morton Landon Translation Award, Academy of American Poets *2014*

International Zbigniew Herbert Literary Award *2013*

Kenyon Review Award for Literary Achievement *2010*

United States Poet Laureate *2010–11*

Pulitzer Prize for Poetry *2009*

Golden Plate Award, American Academy of Achievement *2008*

Ambassador Book Award for Poetry *2006*

Rebekah Johnson Bobbitt National Prize for Poetry, Library of Congress *2006*

National Book Award for Poetry *2005* (nominated five times)

Golden Wreath Award of Struga Poetry Evenings Festival in Macedonia *2004*

Lannan Literary Award for Lifetime Achievement *2004*

Gold Medal for Poetry, American Academy of Arts and Letters *2003*

Ruth Lilly Poetry Prize, Poetry Foundation *1998*

Wallace Stevens Award (Tanning Prize), Academy of American Poets *1994*

Governor's Award for Literature of the State of Hawaii *1987*

Bollingen Prize for Poetry, Yale University Library *1979*

Guggenheim Fellowship *1973*

Pulitzer Prize for Poetry *1971*

PEN Translation Prize (PEN/Book-of-the-Month Club Translation Prize) *1969*

Yale Series of Younger Poets *1952*

About the Editor

Michael Wiegers is the Editor-in-Chief of Copper Canyon Press, where he has edited and published over 300 collections of poetry.

He is the editor of two retrospective volumes of the poetry of Frank Stanford, *What About This* (a finalist for the 2015 National Book Critics Circle Award and winner of the 2015 Balcones Prize) and *Hidden Water* (with Chet Weise), and of *Reversible Monuments: Contemporary Mexican Poetry* (with Mónica de la Torre), *This Art,* and *The Poet's Child.* He additionally serves as Poetry Editor for *Narrative* magazine and translates Spanish-language poetry. He lives in Port Townsend, Washington.

Index

Donors to the Publication

Anonymous (3)
Samuel Alexander
Roseanna Almaee
Lou Amyx
Croil James Anderson
Richard Andrews
Peggy and Jerry Armstrong
Pauline and Robbie Bach
Peter Badame
Jenny Bailey
Jasper Bangs
Roger Barbee
Remi Barbier
Anne Barker
Rochelle and Herbert Bass
Jeffery Beam
Joseph Bednarik
Lauren Bennett
Allison Beondé
Kitty Berger
Erica and Erik Bergmann
Rob Berretta
Linda Bierds and Sydney Kaplan
Greg Bishop
John Wolfe Blotzer
Tara Bloyd
Peter Bodlaender
Kathy Anne and Keith Boi

Michael Bonebrake
Kate Borland
David Bottoms
Charles Boyce
Margot Bradford
Amy Brandt
Joe Bratcher
Stephen and Laurie Brittain
Michael Broomfield
Louise Brown
Michael Dennis Browne
Deborah Buchanan and
        Scott Teitsworth
Vincent T. Buck
Kathleen Burgess
Ralph Calder
Steven Caplow
Mary Carlson
Frank Carsey
Mary Carswell and Mary Berle
Justin P. Cerenzia
Margaret Chillingworth and
        Barry Ziker
Justin Chimka
Nathan Clum
Michael and Katharine Cohen
Bonnie Gaia Colby
Nancy M. Collins-Warner

Elisabeth Colt
Lisa Colt
Keith Comer
The Conn Family
Janet and Les Cox
Constance Crawford
Pete Curran, Betsey Curran, and
    Jonathan King
David Curry
Paula Dax
Eric Deitchman
Curtis Derrick
Kevin J. Doherty
Vasiliki Dwyer
Andy Eaton
Catherine Edwards
Peggy and Alan Ellis
Betty Jean Esveldt
Melissa and Peter Evans
Valerie Eves
Jenny Factor
Beroz Ferrell
Martha Fitzgerald
Kelly Forsythe
Julie Fowler
Matt Garson
Linda Fay Gerrard and
    Walter Parsons
Ros and C. Curtis Ghan
Katharine Gilbert
Jack Gillmar
Cora Blake Godbout
Sierra Golden
Jeff Gordinier

Kristin and Kingdon Gould III
Kip and Stanley Greenthal
Teresa L. Gregory and Jon M.
    Shumaker
Drew E. Griffin
Janice and William Griffin
Michelle Grondine, Robert
    F. Grondine, and Aiko
    Grondine
Deborah Gunn
Elizabeth Guthrie
Josephine Hadlock-King
Eleanor and Gary Hamilton
Dan Harrington
Constance W. Hassett and James
    Richardson
Barry Hathaway
Chris Higashi
Jane Hirshfield
Laura Hirschfield
Adina Hoffman and Peter Cole
Meg Holgate and Bruce Bradburn
James Howe and Mark Davis
Holly Hughes and John Pierce
Cliff Hume
Kathryn Hunt
Katy Hutchins
Paul and Anna Isaacs
Katherine Anne Janeway and
    Howard S. Wright
Duane Kirby Jensen
David Johnson
Susan C. Johnston and Brian J.
    Johnston

Helen K. Jones

Kristen Jorgensen

Pat Juell

Atis Jurka

Timothy Jursak

David Kader

Victoria Kaplan

Charles and Roberta Katz

Richard Katz

Edmund Keeley

Brian Kennan

Susan M. Kerr

Claire Keyes

Susan J. Kilgore and
    Dale D. Goble

Mary Jane Knecht

Tricia Knoll

George Knotek

Taroh Kogure

Despina Kotis

Marty Krasney

Marilyn and Robert Larson

Jon Lasser

Cory Lavender

Rebecca Jill Leaver

Maureen Lee and Mark Busto

James Lenfestey

Takako and Thomas Lento

Sai Li

Jayne Lindley

Jane Lipman

Lee Ann MacDonald

Monica Macguire

Prakash Mackay

Jaclyn Madden

Sallie Rose Madrone

Leslie and Jon Maksik

Russell Marcum

Kara and Ken Masters

David Ira Mayberg

Judy and Howard M. McCue III

Robert McDonnell

In memory of Brendan McManus

Tanya and Michael McManus

Paul McShane

Phillippe and Marian Meany

Katherine Meyer

Laura and David Midgley

Michael Miller

Patti Klumpp Miller

Diana Morley

Joseph P. Morra

Ruth M. Moser

Christopher Charles Miller

Edward W. Mudd, Jr.

Joan Murphy

Julie Murphy

Patricia Nerison

Samantha Neukom

Peter Newland

Julie and Erik Nordstrom

Eugene O'Brien

Susan O'Connor

Resnick Ohana

Chris Okuda

Kurt Olsson

Kisha Palmer

H. Stewart Parker

Marion Patterson

Mickey Pearson

In memory of Karen Kenney Pharr

Simon Phipps

Scott Pomfret

Anne Pound

Nancy and Kelly Price

Dean Rader

Larry Rafferty

Sara and Tripp Ritter

Catherine Roach

Barbara Robinette

Robert H. Roggeveen

Jeffery D. Ross

William G. Ross, Jr.

Ellen and Arthur Rubenfield

Jeannie and William J.
     Ruckelshaus

Pamela J. Sampel

Victoria A. Sanz

Marsie Scharlatt

Susie Schlesinger

Miriam Lynne Schuster

Ammel Sharon

David Shearer

Marsha and John Shyer

Marjorie Simon

Michael Smallwood

Mary Kay Sneeringer and
     David Brewster

Sandra Sohr

Anthony Sparvier

Stephen Spencer

Byron Springer

Frank Stackhouse

Timothy Standal

Jenepher Stowell

Karen Sullivan

Kim and George Suyama

Tree Swenson

James B. Swinerton

Stevens Van Strum

Christian Teresi

Dawn Tripp

Patrick J. Vaz

Lisa Verhovek and Sam Howe

Waverly Paige Wahbeh

Megan Welch

Elizabeth A. Wells

Heide and Jon Wenrick

Paul Eric Wenzel

Reese White and Lorin Yin

Jan and Bob Whitsitt

Michael Wiegers

Barbara Wight and Don Stutheit

Ronald and Melanie Wilensky

Carl R. Wirth

Jason Wirth

Stephen George Wood

Matthew Woodman

Paul Woodruff

Sara and Ted Woolsey

Joan and Craig Wrench

Emily M. Wright

Jennifer and Scott Wyatt

William Young

Sarah Zale and Michael Hindes

Eric Zigman

Poetry is vital to language and living. Since 1972, Copper Canyon Press has published extraordinary poetry from around the world to engage the imaginations and intellects of readers, writers, booksellers, librarians, teachers, students, and donors.

WE ARE GRATEFUL FOR THE MAJOR SUPPORT PROVIDED BY:

THE PAUL G. ALLEN
FAMILY FOUNDATION

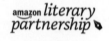

TO LEARN MORE ABOUT UNDERWRITING
COPPER CANYON PRESS TITLES,
PLEASE CALL 360-385-4925 EXT. 103

WE ARE GRATEFUL FOR THE MAJOR SUPPORT PROVIDED BY:

Anonymous

Jill Baker and Jeffrey Bishop

Donna and Matt Bellew

John Branch

Diana Broze

Sarah and Tim Cavanaugh

Janet and Les Cox

Mimi Gardner Gates

Linda Gerrard and Walter Parsons

Gull Industries, Inc. on behalf of
Ruth and William True

The Trust of Warren A. Gummow

Steven Myron Holl

Phil Kovacevich and Eric Wechsler

Lakeside Industries, Inc.
on behalf of Jeanne Marie Lee

Maureen Lee and Mark Busto

Rhoady Lee and Alan Gartenhaus

Ellie Mathews and Carl Youngmann
as The North Press

Anne O'Donnell and John Phillips

Petunia Charitable Fund and
advisor Elizabeth Hebert

Suzie Rapp and Mark Hamilton

Joseph C. Roberts

Jill and Bill Ruckelshaus

Cynthia Lovelace Sears and
Frank Buxton

Kim and Jeff Seely

Catherine Eaton Skinner and
David Skinner

Dan Waggoner

Austin Walters

Barbara and Charles Wright

The dedicated interns and
faithful volunteers of
Copper Canyon Press

The Chinese character for poetry is made up of two parts:
"word" and "temple." It also serves as pressmark for
Copper Canyon Press.

The poems are set in Garamond Premier Pro.
Printed on archival-quality paper.
Book design and composition by Phil Kovacevich.